A Good Day for

Soup

BY JEANNETTE FERRARY AND LOUISE FISZER

CHRONICLE BOOKS
SAN FRANCISCO

LIBRARY OF CONGRESS CATALOGING-IN-PUBLICATION DATA
Ferrary, Jeannette, 1941-
A good day for soup / by Jeannette Ferrary, Louise Fiszer.
p. cm.
Includes index.
ISBN 0-8118-0467-4
1. Soups.   I. Fiszer, Louise.   II. Title.
TX757.F49   1995
641.8'13—dc20   94—43510
CIP

Printed in the United States of America.
Distributed in Canada by Raincoast Books, 8680 Cambie St., Vancouver, B.C. V6P 6M9

10 9 8 7 6 5 4 3 2

Chronicle Books | 85 Second Street | San Francisco, CA 94105

Web Site: www.chronbooks.com

dedi-
cation

To Max and Peter, our "Soupermen"

Table of Contents

A Good Day for

When we were kids, soup was always a treat. Even if it was Campbell's Vegetable—*especially* if it was Campbell's Vegetable!—we greeted soup with the anticipation and delight that were eventually to make Andy Warhol a fortune. Because of its wide appeal, American food makers soon translated soup into every conceivable form: boxed, dehydrated, vacuum-packed, cubed, powdered, precupped, bagged, frozen, microwavable. Even so, it is not rare to find someone who has never tasted homemade soup. A friend told us he once bought a box of chicken soup and was amused that its package promised it would taste just like his mother used to make.

"Unfortunately, it did!," he reported with dismay, realizing that the instant version was exactly what his mother used to make.

The recent rediscovery of fresh ingredients and healthy but delicious dishes has brought soup back into the limelight. Soup can incorporate all the food groups in one dish. It can be easy or complicated, long simmering or almost instant, rich or light. And it still allows the busy cook to take advantage of the contemporary marketplace by judiciously combining, for example, farmers' market tomatoes and backyard basil with canned cannellini beans and one of today's much improved canned broths.

There is nothing so sensitive to today's diverse and demanding lifestyles as soup. It is the answer to the problems of fussy kids and even fussier adults, to minimal cooking skills, to belt-tightening budgets that require stretchable, economical, downright cheap stone soups. It meets the necessity of accommodating various tastes and preferences at one single dinner table; of time constraints; of health and diet considerations; of the need for freezable, easy, make ahead, quick-to-prepare, stressless, reheatable, even unwatched soups. Soup is about the only thing we know that can delight the dieter, the vegetarian, the pragmatist, the sensualist, the health nut, hurriers, worriers, even noncooks. In fact, soup may well be the pasta of the nineties.

JEANNETTE FERRARY AND LOUISE FISZER

In order to make this book as helpful and accessible as possible, each chapter is devoted to a specific situation or problem. A glance at the contents illustrates how this arrangement is carried out, beginning with the Blueprint for Soups, which includes many types of stocks and even a few shortcuts. The soups in Soups for Starters make an easy beginning for a meal, special and intriguing first courses. Dinner in a Bowl provides easy and economical one-pot meals. Entertaining Soups are tailored to special occasions, such as buffets, holiday gatherings, outdoor festivities, and so on. Cold and Cookless Soups are full of refreshing first-course and dessert soups that require little or no cooking. Slendersoups are low in fat but high in flavor, offering new techniques for creamless but creamy-tasting soups. Recycled Soups are clean-out-the-fridge meals from leftover pasta, risotto, cooked veggies, and the like. Folksoups are traditional, nostalgia-inducing soups given new twists for contemporary tastes. Finally the Soupçons chapter contains an array of easy-to-prepare breads, scones, biscuits, and soup accompaniments.

Note: Because elderly people, pregnant women, and those with immune deficiencies have been advised not to eat raw or undercooked eggs due to the possible presence of bacteria, they should not use recipes containing them.

In the course of doing this book, we inadvertently discovered the informal science of soupography. It all started quite unexpectedly whenever we said we were writing a book about soup. "Ah, yes, soup . . ." people would say in a kind of dreamy voice and then start talking about the soup they used to cook back in Wisconsin or how their Sicilian grandmother could make fantastic soup with only stale bread. Once they began reminiscing, there was no stopping them; soup led seamlessly to warm recollections of childhood and favorite family meals, memories of ethnic heritage and personal lifestyle. Which is what we mean by soupography:

the ability of a conversation about soup to reveal so much about so many aspects of people's lives. Once we discovered soupography, we decided to fill our book with the kinds of anecdotes, evocative recipes, and background notes that get people sipping and reminiscing with unbridled enthusiasm.

So if you talk to someone about soup, be prepared; if you go one step farther and actually serve someone soup, you may be amazed at the response! Meanwhile, here are some of the spontaneous revelations that followed the mere mention of the word:

(continued)

A GOOD DAY FOR SOUP

"I'm a soup enthusiast. About once a year I make a soup and I hardly ever repeat it. I don't exactly love cooking, but something builds up in me, I don't know what, and then I can't control myself. It just comes out!"

"I always remember the soups my mother made and what we had with them—the cornbread with the oxtail soup. And with the bean soup we put in some catsup."

"My mother used to make wonderful soups, and you know, she had a secret. She would add little pieces of butternut squash and by the time the soup was ready, they would almost disappear. But they were there all right. That's what gave her soups their special taste. The turkey and rice, the minestra, even the pea soup."

"I think there's a connection between soup and language. You know the way immigrants try to keep the language alive in their children and grandchildren after they come here. I think the same thing happens with soup. After a while, everything becomes assimilated; by the third generation, it's not ethnic anymore."

"My grandmother used to say you can tell how good a restaurant is by its soup. If the soup is good, the rest of the food is probably all right too. Anyway, I love soup—Greek chicken, lemon—and pistou; I think I knew pistou before I knew pesto."

"So here's the basic recipe for Turkey White Bean Chili. My variations often include celery, fresh mushrooms, and diced red pepper. I actually made a pot yesterday and as I write this I'm getting hungry, so good-bye for now. I have to go eat!"

"Ah, yes, soup…There was a place on the east side back in New York. Used to make the best pastafazool. I've looked everywhere for a recipe. If I could find a recipe for pastafazool, I'd make it every day."

ELENA S., PHOTOGRAPHER,
SAN FRANCISCO

"Over the holidays I found a bag of mixed beans. The bag had a recipe on it called bean bouillabaisse. I never found the bag again, so now I make it my own way."

RANNA M., MUSIC
TEACHER, SAN MATEO

"I always wanted to have a souper party. I'd make the stock and put it on the stove. Everyone would come with their favorite vegetable and just throw it in. People could do wild things with their vegetable—spiral the carrots, use a cookie cutter on potatoes, curlicue the zucchini."

JOHN L., MUSIC STUDENT,
STANFORD

"Before my mother died, she never got around to giving us what we called her National Monument Soup. It was made with beef and rice and lima beans. I used to make such a fuss about my mother's soup that my wife once said 'It's just soup, for God's sake. It's not a national monument!'"

LEONARD R., MUSICIAN AND PROFESSOR,
STANFORD

"Every soup is different. I think since the beginning of time no two soups have ever been the same. Except perhaps for Campbell's."

PETER C., HISTORIAN

Quotes Captain James M. Sanderson in Camp Fires and Camp Cooking *(Government Printing Office, 1862)*
"Kitchen Philosophy: Remember that beans, badly boiled, kill more than bullets; and fat is more fatal than powder. In cooking, more than anything else in this world, always make haste slowly. One hour too much is vastly better than five minutes too little, with rare exceptions. A big fire scorches your soup, burns your face, and crisps your temper."

blue-
print

for soups

Like all adages, the one about good soup beginning with good stock is true. If the stock isn't flavorful and balanced, the soup can't come out right, no matter how exotic or expensive or trendy the ingredients that go into it. The following stocks are excellent starts for any soup recipe anywhere.

In this book, the most commonly used is chicken stock, which is easily accessible and handy to make. But if you've simmered up a great homemade veal stock, and the recipe you want to make seems compatible, by all means substitute. Likewise, unless otherwise indicated, our vegetable stock can always be substituted, especially in recipes without any meat ingredients. For those blitz days, when there's no time at all, we also include a pantry stock, which makes use of canned stock or clam juice.

The care and cooking of beans and legumes is also included in this chapter because they are among our favorite ingredients for nutrition, taste, and just plain goodness. When recipes call for cooked beans, you can always use canned. But the taste of beans cooked from scratch, either by the overnight or quick-soak method, compensates for the extra time.

CHICKEN STOCK

2 pounds mixed chicken parts, such as necks,
   wings, and backs
1 onion, cut into small pieces
1 leek, thoroughly washed and sliced
2 carrots, sliced
1 clove garlic (optional)
1 stalk celery, sliced
1 bay leaf
6 sprigs parsley

In a large stockpot, combine all ingredients and cover with cold water by at least 3 inches. Bring to a gentle boil and skim grayish foam that forms on surface. Continue to skim until this foam no longer forms. Reduce heat and simmer, uncovered, for 2 hours. Strain into storage containers, let cool, and refrigerate. Remove solidified fat from surface.

Makes about 8 cups

SIMPLE BEEF STOCK

---

2 pounds beef bones
2 pounds beef stew meat
1 onion, halved, and each half stuck with
* 1 whole clove*
1 leek, thoroughly washed and sliced
2 stalks celery, sliced
2 cloves garlic
6 sprigs parsley
2 bay leaves
½ teaspoon dried thyme
6 peppercorns

In a large stockpot, combine all ingredients and cover with cold water by at least 3 inches. Bring to a gentle boil and skim grayish foam that forms on surface. Continue to skim until this foam no longer appears. Reduce heat and simmer about 2 hours. Remove meat and continue to simmer another 3 hours. (Meat will be rather tasteless and stringy—feed to pets or discard.) Strain into storage containers, let cool, and refrigerate. Remove solidified fat from surface.

Makes about 8 cups

BROWN BEEF STOCK

3 tablespoons oil
3 pounds beef bones
2 pounds beef stew meat
2 stalks celery, cut into 3-inch pieces
1 onion, halved
2 carrots, sliced
3 cloves garlic
3 sprigs parsley
2 bay leaves
½ teaspoon dried thyme
6 peppercorns

Preheat the oven to 400 degrees F. In a roasting pan large enough to hold all the ingredients, spread the oil. Add bones and meat and turn to coat with oil. Roast 30 minutes. Add vegetables, herbs, and spices and roast 1 more hour. Transfer vegetables, meat, and bones to large stockpot. Add about 1 cup water to roasting pan and deglaze, scraping up the brown bits sticking to bottom of pan, over medium heat on top of stove. Pour this liquid into stockpot along with enough cold water to cover by at least 3 inches. Bring to a gentle boil, skimming any grayish foam that forms on surface.

Simmer gently, uncovered, about 4 hours. Strain into storage containers, let cool, and refrigerate. Remove solidified fat from surface.

Makes about 12 cups

1 can (10 ounces) reduced-sodium chicken or
*   beef stock or clam juice*
1 stalk celery, sliced
1 carrot, sliced
1 onion, sliced
3 sprigs parsley
1 bay leaf
½ cup white wine
3 cups water

In a medium stockpot, combine all ingredients. Bring to a boil, reduce heat, and simmer gently for 30 minutes. Strain into storage containers, let cool, and refrigerate. (There should be no fat in this method.)

Makes about 4 cups

FISH STOCK

2 pounds bones from white-fleshed, nonoily
  fish, rinsed under cold water
½ cup white wine
3 tablespoons chopped shallots
1 carrot, sliced
1 stalk celery, sliced
3 sprigs parsley
½ teaspoon dried thyme
3 peppercorns
6 cups water

In a medium stockpot, combine all ingredients. Bring to a gentle boil, skimming any foam that forms on surface. Reduce heat and simmer 30 minutes. Strain into storage containers and refrigerate.

Makes about 6 cups

VEGETABLE STOCK

2 stalks celery, with leaves, chopped
4 carrots, chopped
2 onions, chopped
1 leek, thoroughly washed and chopped
1 large tomato, quartered (optional)
1 small head lettuce, cored and shredded
2 cabbage leaves, shredded
6 sprigs parsley
1 bay leaf
½ teaspoon dried thyme
1-inch strip of lemon zest (optional)
8 cups water

In a medium stockpot, combine all ingredients. Bring to a gentle boil and skim gray foam that forms on surface. Reduce heat and simmer gently for 1 hour. Strain into storage containers, let cool, and refrigerate.

Makes about 6 cups

MUSHROOM STOCK

¼ cup (1 ounce) dried mushrooms, soaked in
* hot water for 30 minutes*
1 small onion, chopped
½ pound fresh mushrooms, chopped
1 carrot, chopped
1 stalk celery, chopped
½ small fennel bulb, chopped
6 sprigs parsley
½ teaspoon dried tarragon
1 tablespoon tomato paste
6 cups water

Strain the soaked mushrooms, reserving liquid. Rinse to remove any grit that may be clinging to them and chop. Place in a medium stockpot. Add remaining ingredients. Strain reserved mushroom liquid and add to pot with the water. Bring to a gentle boil, skimming gray foam that forms on surface. Simmer gently for 45 minutes. Strain into storage containers, let cool, and refrigerate.

Makes about 6 cups

LIGHT VEAL OR LAMB STOCK

1 pound lamb or veal stew meat, cut into very
   small pieces or chopped
1 carrot, chopped
1 small onion, chopped
1 clove garlic
1 stalk celery, chopped
½ teaspoon dried thyme
3 sprigs parsley
1 bay leaf
1 fresh tomato, cut into eighths

In a large nonreactive stockpot, combine all ingredients. Add enough cold water to cover by 2 inches. Bring to a simmer, skimming gray foam that comes to surface. Simmer over low heat about 1 hour. Strain into storage containers, let cool, and refrigerate. Remove solidified fat from surface.

Makes about 8 cups

TOMATO STOCK

---

1 small onion, chopped
2 garlic cloves, peeled
3 pounds ripe tomatoes, chopped
1 stalk celery, chopped
¼ cup tomato paste
1 teaspoon sugar
3 sprigs parsley
1 sprig thyme or ½ teaspoon dried thyme
1 bay leaf
6 cups water

In a large nonreactive stockpot, combine ingredients. Bring to a gentle boil, skimming foam that forms on surface. Simmer 45 minutes. Strain into storage containers, let cool, and refrigerate.

Makes about 6 cups

CLARIFIED STOCK

Stock that is made properly will be clear enough for most purposes. Skimming the foam and simmering—not boiling the stock—will insure clarity. Some soups, such as consommés, should be crystal clear. To clarify strained stock, in a large stockpot combine 2 crushed egg shells, 2 egg whites, 1 small chopped onion, 1 diced carrot, ½ stalk celery, and 1 ice cube. Pour in cold strained stock. Cook over high heat, stirring constantly until mixture comes to a boil. The egg white mixture will form a white crust on top. Simmer for 20 minutes; crust will collect all the particles in the stock. Make a hole in the center of the crust. Place ladle in hole and ladle stock into a strainer set over a bowl. Stock should be crystal clear.

EQUIPMENT

Stockpot. A good stockpot should have a heavy bottom and two side handles for easy carrying as it gets heavy when full. It should be tall and narrow to avoid excessive evaporation.

Skimmer. The tool most efficient for skimming surface foam from the stock is indeed called a skimmer. It should be of a good quality stainless steel, with a fine mesh, and no larger than 6 inches in diameter.

Fine-mesh strainer. A large strainer with a very fine mesh should be used for straining stock.

Blender or food processor. These make quick work of puréeing soups. The blender gives a smoother finished product than a food processor.

Food mill. This hand tool may be used instead of, or in addition to, a food processor or blender to produce the smoothest of textures. For example, after puréeing a pea soup in the blender or food processor, it should be put through a food mill to remove all traces of pea skins and membranes.

INGREDIENTS

Making good stock or soup is an inexact science. The following guidelines help.

Water. The proportion of water to the rest of the ingredients is never exact. A good guideline is to cover the loosely packed ingredients by 2 to 3 inches of water.

Vegetables. Use only fresh, good quality ingredients. Don't scavenge the far corners of your refrigerator for past-their-prime vegetables to put in stock. Your stock will reflect whatever you put in.

Meat. Trim meat and poultry of visible fat. Rinse bones under cold water.

Flavoring. Salt and pepper should be added when stock is used for the actual soup. Because evaporation takes place during stock making, the flavor of salt would be intensified and overpowering.

BOILING VS SIMMERING

Once the initial boil has taken place, immediately turn the heat down so that the stock simmers for the remainder of the cooking time. Boiling causes the solids to disintegrate, making the stock muddy. Boiling also causes the fat in the meat to break down and form a stable emulsion. This will make your stock greasy and the fat impossible to remove.

STORAGE

Strain the finished stock into refrigerator or freezer storage containers. A capacity of 1 to 2 quarts is ideal. Let the stock cool and refrigerate overnight. The fat will rise to the top and become solidified, making it easy to remove by lifting it off.

Cover the stock and refrigerate up to 3 days. If stock is to be kept longer than 3 days in the refrigerator, it must be brought to a boil, allowed to cool, and refrigerated again. Stock may be kept in the freezer up to 4 months.

Lentils and split peas need only a thorough rinsing before they are cooked. Beans and whole peas must be soaked in water after they are rinsed. There are two ways to do this.

Overnight Soak Immerse the beans in cold water—about 3 cups of water for every cup of beans. Soak 8 hours or overnight. Drain beans and discard water. Place beans in a heavy pot with 3 cups of cold water for every cup of beans. Water should cover beans by at least 1 inch. Bring to a boil, skimming off foam that rises to surface. Boil for about 10 minutes, reduce heat, and simmer, covered, until beans are tender, 30 minutes to 1 hour depending on bean. Drain and use as directed in recipe.

Quick Soak Place the beans in a heavy pot with 3 cups cold water for each cup of beans. Boil, uncovered, for 2 minutes. Remove from heat, cover, and set aside to soak for 1 hour. Drain and cook as in overnight soak method.

TOASTING AND ROASTING INGREDIENTS

Roasting Peppers: Place peppers over a gas burner, under a broiler, or on a barbecue grill. Roast until skin blisters and blackens, turning peppers often. Place in a plastic bag until cool enough to handle and scrape skin away with a small paring knife.

Toasting Nuts: Spread desired amount of nuts or seeds on a cookie sheet and place in a pre-heated oven at 350 degrees for about 10 minutes, shaking pan once during that time. Nuts and seeds should be no darker than a light, golden brown.

NOTES

NOTES

First course.

Soup for starters

As the official beginning of the meal, the first course is supposed to turn on the lights, gastronomically. Perhaps nothing alerts the taste buds and starts the juices flowing so efficiently as soup. With the wild smokiness of roasted red peppers, the sharp buzz of chopped jalapeños, the seductive warmth of fennel, these starter soups entice and tease and provoke the palate. Not bad for a beginning.

first course.

Staleness has always been welcome by the creative cook—and by the creative anybody. (What else is junk sculpture but the result of an artist's gambol in a scrap heap of discards? Indeed the very word *nostalgia* seems to have "stale" embedded in it.) So it's no wonder that kitchen wizards everywhere look forward to yesterday's bread. Catalans rub it with tomato and olive oil and maybe a bit of anchovy to make *pa amb tomaquet*. *Pain perdu* has brightened up many an otherwise crusty morning. And anyone with a sharp knife can bake up a batch of fresh croutons. Slices of stale bread add immeasurably to soups, especially when they're crowned with a sprinkle of Parmesan. Whatever you do, this soup, with its lush, green asparagus, tastes as new as spring.

---

3 tablespoons canola or vegetable oil or butter
¼ pound prosciutto, diced
¼ cup chopped shallots
½ teaspoon dried tarragon or 1 teaspoon
  chopped fresh tarragon leaves
4 cups Chicken Stock (page 20)
2 pounds asparagus, trimmed, peeled, and
  cut into 1-inch pieces

1 cup heavy cream or half-and-half
Salt and pepper

PARMESAN TOASTS
12 slices baguette, toasted
¾ cup (3 ounces) grated Parmesan cheese

In a medium saucepan, heat oil over medium-high heat. Cook prosciutto until golden brown, about 5 minutes. Remove and reserve. Add shallots and cook until soft, about 3 minutes. Stir in tarragon and stock. Bring to a boil and add asparagus. Simmer, uncovered, until asparagus is tender, about 10 minutes.

Meanwhile make Parmesan toasts by sprinkling each baguette slice with grated cheese. Put under the broiler until cheese is bubbly and melted. Set aside.

In a food processor or blender, purée soup with cream. Return to pot and stir in prosciutto. Taste for salt and pepper. Reheat if necessary and serve with Parmesan toasts.

Serves 6

SUGAR SNAP PEA SOUP WITH ORZO AND MINT

When it comes to pea soup, this one is nothing like what mama used to make. In fact, some of our mamas never heard of Sugar Snap peas, which haven't been around that long. They were developed quite deliberately about fifteen years ago as a "correction" of the snow pea, which commercial processors found difficult to process because its pods were too flexible. At the Gallatin Valley Seed Company in Twin Falls, Idaho, a man named Calvin Lamborn crossed green peas and snow peas in an attempt to produce a sturdier variety. What he got turned out to be sweeter, plumper, and more succulent than either of its forebears. It is also quicker to prepare and cook, giving it a very nineties appeal, as in this easily made first course with its fragrance of mint and nutmeg.

---

3 tablespoons butter
2 leeks, white parts only, thoroughly washed
    and chopped
1 carrot, chopped
½ cup chopped fresh parsley
½ cup orzo
½ teaspoon freshly grated nutmeg
5 cups Chicken Stock (page 20)
¾ pound Sugar Snap peas, strings removed,
    cut into 3 pieces
Salt and pepper
¼ cup chopped fresh mint

In a medium saucepan, heat butter over medium heat. Cook leeks and carrots until soft, about 5 minutes. Stir in parsley and orzo and cook another 3 minutes. Add nutmeg and stock, bring to a boil, and cook about 10 minutes. Add peas and cook another 3 minutes. Taste for salt and pepper, stir in nutmeg and mint, and serve.

Serves 6

For a soup with such simple and inexpensive ingredients, this one always makes a grand entrance. And for good reason. Each bowl is a glow of yellow-orange topped with strips of cilantro ribbons that pique the curiosity like a wrapped package. It can be a taste-provoking beginning to an Indian or Middle Eastern meal.

RIBBONS	SOUP
2 eggs	2 tablespoons vegetable oil
1 tablespoon flour	1 small onion, chopped
1 tablespoon milk	1 stalk celery, chopped
½ teaspoon salt	1 teaspoon curry powder, or to taste
¼ teaspoon freshly ground pepper	½ teaspoon ground coriander
¼ cup fresh cilantro leaves, chopped	2 tablespoons flour
1 tablespoon vegetable oil	5 cups Chicken Stock (page 20)
	1 pound carrots, sliced
	4 tablespoons heavy cream
	Salt and pepper

To make ribbons, in a medium bowl, whisk together eggs, flour, milk, salt, and pepper. Stir in cilantro. In an 8-inch skillet, preferably nonstick, heat oil. Pour in egg mixture, tilting pan back and forth. Cook until batter is set. Turn over to cook other side for 1 minute. Slide onto cutting board and let cool. Cut into thin strips and set aside.

To make soup, in a medium saucepan, heat oil. Add onion and celery and cook until soft. Stir in curry, coriander, and flour and cook another minute. Add stock, bring to a boil and add carrots. Simmer, partly covered, 15 minutes. In a blender or food processor, purée the mixture with cream. Taste for salt and pepper. Divide ribbons among 6 bowls, ladle soup over them, and serve.

Serves 6

SPICY CARROT SOUP WITH SWEET PEA PURÉE

This soup never fails to spark some controversy as guests try to figure out what the green purée is made from. Because of the visual resemblance to guacamole, the first-guessers always jump in with avocado, which would seem appropriate in this jalapeño-speckled dish. Broccoli? Spinach? The discussion can become quite heated. In fact, the lively repartee alone makes this soup a smart choice for the beginning of a meal.

---

2 tablespoons vegetable oil
½ onion, chopped
1 jalapeño pepper, seeded and chopped
2 cloves garlic, minced
⅛ teaspoon cayenne
6 medium carrots, sliced
1 small potato, peeled and diced
5 cups Chicken Stock (page 20) or
   Vegetable Stock (page 25)
¼ cup heavy cream
Salt and pepper

SWEET PEA PURÉE
1½ cups cooked peas
⅓ cup heavy cream
Pinch sugar
Salt and pepper

In a medium saucepan, heat oil over medium-high heat. Cook onion, jalapeño, and garlic until soft, about 5 minutes. Stir in cayenne, carrots, potato, and stock. Simmer, partly covered, 20 minutes.

Meanwhile make pea purée. In a blender or food processor, purée peas and cream. (If you want a very smooth purée, push through fine sieve to eliminate pea skins.) Taste for sugar, salt, and pepper. If peas are not naturally sweet, add sugar to compensate. When soup is done, purée in food processor or blender. Ladle into soup bowls and swirl about ¼ cup of pea purée into each serving.

Serves 6

CARROT AND CAULIFLOWER BISQUE WITH CHIVES

When we called this chive-flecked vegetable soup a bisque, we knew that purists might quarrel. Some say that bisque originally referred to a seafood dish, thickened with egg yolks and cream and finished off with a big splash of brandy or sherry. But such eminent authorities as *Le Cuisinier méthodique* (1662) insist that bisques begin with a rich multimeat stock and end with a final garnishing of exotica, such as sweetbreads and cockscombs. These days, however, the trend to "vegetablize" everything from beef stroganov to hamburgers may sometimes seem extreme. But the resulting revisions, such as this bisque, with its pale carrot-orange hue, are often healthier as well as fresher tasting, more flavorful—and pretty.

---

3 tablespoons butter or vegetable oil
1 leek, white part only, thoroughly washed
  and chopped
1 teaspoon ground cumin
½ teaspoon ground coriander
5 cups Chicken Stock (page 20) or Vegetable
  Stock (page 25)
4 medium carrots, chopped
2 cups cauliflower florets
1 small potato, peeled and diced
½ cup sour cream
Salt and pepper
½ cup chopped chives

In a medium saucepan, heat butter over medium-high heat. Cook leek until soft, about 5 minutes. Stir in cumin and coriander and cook until fragrant, about 2 minutes. Add stock, carrots, cauliflower, and potato. Simmer, partly covered, 20 minutes. Purée in a food processor or blender. Whisk in the sour cream. Taste for salt and pepper. Serve, sprinkled with chives.

Serves 6

CREAM OF CHESTNUT AND CARROT SOUP

This recipe was inspired by none other than the great German poet Johann Goethe, who wrote admiringly of the chestnut in his *Prose Maxims* as one of the "noble products of the earth." He liked his chopped up and cooked with glazed sweetened turnips. Here the carrots and honey provide the sweetness to contrast with and complement the deep chestnut taste. As for the chopped chestnut garnish, it's positively, well, poetic.

2 tablespoons butter
2 leeks, thoroughly washed and sliced
½ teaspoon ground cinnamon
½ teaspoon grated nutmeg
1 teaspoon honey
6 carrots, sliced
2 cups peeled chestnuts, fresh, canned, or
  vacuum-packed
4 cups Chicken Stock (page 20)
½ cup fresh chervil leaves
1 cup heavy cream
Salt and pepper

In a medium saucepan, heat butter over medium-high heat. Cook leeks until soft, about 6 minutes, and stir in cinnamon, nutmeg, and honey. Cook another minute. Add carrots, all but 6 chestnuts, and stock. Bring to a boil and simmer partly covered, 25 minutes.

Meanwhile, quarter the reserved 6 chestnuts and brown in a dry skillet, over medium heat, about 4 minutes. Chop coarsely with chervil leaves and set aside. Purée soup with cream. Taste for salt and pepper. Garnish each serving with a sprinkling of chestnut-chervil mixture.

Serves 6

True confit is gastronomy's most elegant and irresistible version of grease. Classic confit is made with pieces of marinated goose, duck, or pork cooked and preserved in its own fat. In French homes, an earthenware crock of *confit d'oie* (or *de canard,* or *de porc*) can usually be found aging gently in the coolness of the wine cellar. Vegetable confits are noble, new creations fit for the central heating and city sidewalks most of us inhabit today. In this eggplant confit, seasoned chopped vegetables melt together into a thick savory jam preserved not with fat but with vinegar. The confit adds interest and complexity to this red pepper soup and is also delicious as a spread or sauce.

SOUP

2 tablespoons olive oil

½ onion, chopped

5 large red bell peppers, seeded and chopped

1 cup chopped tomatoes

1 fennel bulb, trimmed and chopped

1 teaspoon fresh thyme leaves or ½ teaspoon
    dried thyme

1 teaspoon sweet paprika

1 teaspoon sugar

5 cups Chicken Stock (page 20)

½ cup sour cream

Salt and pepper

CONFIT

3 tablespoons olive oil

1 medium onion, chopped

2 cloves garlic, thinly sliced

1 medium eggplant, diced

1 zucchini, diced

½ cup chopped tomatoes

½ teaspoon fennel seed

½ teaspoon dried oregano

¼ cup balsamic vinegar

Salt and pepper

To make the confit, heat the oil in a nonreactive skillet over medium-high heat. Add onions and garlic and cook over medium heat until onions are soft, about 5 minutes. Add eggplant and zucchini and cook until soft, about 5 minutes. Stir in tomatoes, fennel seed, and oregano and cook until mixture becomes thick and most of the moisture is evaporated, 10 to 12 minutes. Add vinegar and cook until almost no liquid is left in pan. Mixture should be jamlike. Taste for salt and pepper and remove to serving dish. You should have about 2 cups. Confit will keep about 2 weeks, well covered, in refrigerator.

To make the soup, heat oil in a large heavy nonreactive pot. Add onion and red peppers and cook, covered, until vegetables are soft, about 5 minutes. Stir in tomatoes, fennel, thyme, paprika and sugar and simmer about 10 minutes. Pass mixture through a food mill and return to pot with stock and sour cream. Mix thoroughly and heat through. Taste for salt and pepper. Serve with a dollop of eggplant confit.

Serves 6

When it comes to making soup, even the most self-assured cook has always had a little trouble with fresh corn. What everyone wants, of course, is to capture the elusive sweetness of just-picked corn in the form of an interesting, tasty soup or chowder. Old recipes tried to accomplish this by long, slow cooking, an hour or longer, cobs and all. Seasonings, herbs, and spices were strictly prohibited except for an imperceptible shake of salt and pepper. (One daring recipe did allow a slice of onion, but it was to be removed discreetly after a suitable interval.) This modern-day rendition, with its zing of cilantro and bright glints of red pepper, seems suited to more vigorous times.

---

3 tablespoons butter or oil
2 red bell peppers, seeded and chopped
6 scallions, trimmed and chopped
1 tablespoon ground cumin
4 cups corn kernels, fresh, or frozen and thawed
2 cups milk
2½ cups Chicken Stock (page 20)
4 small red new potatoes, diced
½ cup grated cheddar or jack cheese
Salt and pepper
½ cup cilantro leaves, for garnish

In a large pot, heat the butter over medium heat. Cook peppers and scallions until soft, about 5 minutes. Stir in cumin. In a blender or food processor, process 2 cups corn with milk until fairly smooth. Add pepper mixture. Add stock and bring to a boil. Add potatoes and let simmer until potatoes are tender, about 10 minutes. Stir in cheese, simmer, stirring, another 3 minutes. Taste for salt and pepper and serve garnished with cilantro.

Serves 6

CHICKEN SOUP WITH CHILI CUSTARDS

Over the centuries, the world's many cultures have come up with all sorts of puffs, dumplings, crusts, and edible confetti to scatter on top of soup. Russians boil up dumpling-type balls called *kletski* or *galushki* or *pampushki*. The French have *quenelles* and *croûtons* and tiny *gougères*. Germans make pancake strips called *Flädle* to float on clear consommés and dumplings called *Keilchen* and *Kluntjes*. Mexican soups sizzle from the last-minute landings of hot tortilla strips. Czechs have hundreds of dumplings made from everything from liver to bread crumbs. Our addition to the world of toppings can make fascinating conversation pieces, depending on your stock of cookie cutters.

CUSTARD
1 egg
3 egg yolks
4 tablespoons milk
1 jalapeño pepper, seeded and chopped
2 tablespoons chopped fresh cilantro leaves
1 tablespoon tomato paste
¼ teaspoon salt

8 cups Chicken Stock (page 20),
clarified (page 29)

Preheat the oven to 300 degrees F. Grease an 8 x 5-inch loaf pan. Combine custard ingredients until well blended. Pour into loaf pan and place in a larger pan of hot water. Bake until custard is set, about 25 minutes. Allow to cool. Using small cookie cutters, cut out desired shapes. Heat stock and float custard shapes in it.

Serves 8

For those who shy away from cutting little X's in chestnuts, this recipe is a boon. We use chestnut purée, not only for ease of preparation, but also because the soup is eventually puréed anyway. For those who enjoy carving X's, there are still eight fresh chestnuts to roast for the garnish.

---

2 tablespoons butter
¼ cup chopped shallots
2 pounds brussels sprouts, trimmed of outer
  leaves
4 cups Chicken Stock (page 20)
1 can (8 ounces) unsweetened chestnut purée
½ cup heavy cream
¼ teaspoon freshly grated nutmeg
⅛ teaspoon cayenne
¼ cup dry sherry
Salt and pepper
¼ cup chopped fresh parsley
8 fresh chestnuts, roasted, peeled, and chopped

In a medium saucepan, heat butter over medium heat. Cook shallots until soft, about 5 minutes. Stir in brussels sprouts, stock, and chestnut purée. Simmer until sprouts are tender, about 20 minutes. Purée mixture with cream. Return to saucepan and add nutmeg, cayenne, and sherry. Heat through over medium heat and taste for salt and pepper. Sprinkle with parsley and chopped chestnuts and serve.

Serves 8

CABBAGE, APPLE, AND LEEK SOUP

"A familiar kitchen-garden vegetable about as large and wise as a man's head." Such was Ambrose Bierce's definition of the cabbage in his delightfully sardonic *Devil's Dictionary*. The resemblance obviously struck the person who first named the sphere-shaped vegetable since the word *cabbage* comes from the Latin *caput,* meaning "head". Even in Greek times, Aristotle reportedly made a habit of nibbling a bit of cabbage before banquets because he believed it cleared his head. Cabbage has also gained a certain following for its reputed ability to prevent and/or cure intoxication. For this soup, we chose a mix of red and green cabbage, which meld deliciously with apple and fresh ginger.

---

2 tablespoons vegetable oil
2 leeks, white parts only, thoroughly washed
  and chopped
½ head red cabbage, cored and shredded
½ head green cabbage, cored and shredded
2 tablespoons grated fresh ginger
2 tablespoons honey
2 apples, peeled and chopped
1 large tomato, seeded and chopped
6 cups Vegetable Stock (page 25)
Salt and pepper
2 tablespoons fresh mint leaves, chopped

In a nonreactive medium saucepan, heat the oil over medium heat. Cook leeks and cabbage until wilted, about 7 minutes. Stir in ginger, honey, apples, and tomato. Cook, stirring, 5 minutes. Add stock and bring to a boil. Reduce heat and simmer, uncovered, 20 minutes. Taste for salt and pepper. Sprinkle with mint and serve.

Serves 8

Someone once said that if we ate only what was good for us, a healthy dose of broccoli would be on our menus every day. A daily broccoli ration sounds about as appetizing as multiple vitamin pills, and about as reasonable. Some researcher is sure to discover that broccophiles turn green after a while or that they sprout florets in the oddest places. On the other hand, this particular broccoli dish often becomes a favorite of those who wouldn't think of eating any more of that vegetable than absolutely necessary. Probably it's the intoxicating lure of the curry spices— cardamom and coriander, turmeric, mace, et al.—working their magic in this basically simple, quickly made soup.

2 tablespoons vegetable oil
6 scallions, trimmed and chopped
1 stalk celery, chopped
1 tablespoon curry powder, or to taste
1 teaspoon ground cumin
2 tablespoons flour
2 pounds fresh broccoli, stems peeled and
   trimmed, chopped
5 cups Chicken Stock (page 20) or Vegetable
   Stock (page 25)
½ cup heavy cream, half-and-half, or milk
Salt and pepper
½ cup chopped chives

In a medium saucepan, heat oil over medium-high heat. Cook scallions and celery until soft, about 7 minutes. Stir in curry powder, cumin, and flour and cook, stirring, about another minute. Add broccoli and stock, and bring to a boil over high heat. Reduce heat and simmer, uncovered, 15 minutes. Purée with cream in a food processor or blender. Taste for salt and pepper. Garnish with chives and serve.

Serves 6

CUMIN-SCENTED CAULIFLOWER SOUP WITH RED PEPPER STRIPS

The ivory-white innocent-looking cauliflower is one of the garden's most sensuous productions. Its tactile surfaces are invitingly bumpy, both raw and cooked, and the satiny purée it becomes is irresistibly creamy, even in a light soup such as this. The smoky taste of red peppers sets off the flavors here. There is no substitute for the toasted cumin seeds.

---

2 tablespoons cumin seed
2 tablespoons canola or vegetable oil
¼ cup chopped shallots
1 stalk celery, chopped
1 small head cauliflower, broken into small
* pieces*
3 tablespoons rice
5 cups Chicken Stock (page 20)
1 large red bell pepper
Salt and pepper

In a small dry skillet, toast cumin seed over medium heat until it darkens and becomes fragrant, about 5 minutes. Let cool slightly and then grind to a rough powder with a mortar and pestle or in a spice grinder.

In a medium saucepan, heat oil over medium-high heat. Cook shallots and celery until soft, about 6 minutes. Stir in ground cumin and cook about 1 minute. Add cauliflower, rice, and stock. Simmer, partly covered, 20 minutes.

Meanwhile, roast pepper on burner or broiler until charred all over. Place in a bag and let cool. Remove charred skin, stem, and seeds and cut pepper into very thin strips. Set aside. Purée soup and taste for salt and pepper. Stir in pepper strips and serve.

Serves 6

Chick peas, garlic, and lemon—this combination always reminds us of hummus. As an appetizer, a big bowl of that Middle Eastern, garlicky dip, surrounded by sliced pita breads, has probably ruined more dinners than any other single hors d'oeuvre. People can't stop eating it and they don't, which usually spells disaster for the big roast lamb waiting on the carving board. But as a first course, a better choice would be something like this soup, another tribute to the luscious chick pea. While it conveys a bit of that seductive hummus spirit, this starter soup has a lightness that imparts to guests a sense of prelude.

2 tablespoons vegetable oil
½ cup chopped red onion
1 cup quartered button mushrooms
1 pound green beans, trimmed and cut into
    1-inch pieces
6 cups Chicken Stock (page 20) or Vegetable
    Stock (page 25)
2 cups freshly cooked or canned chick peas
2 tablespoons fresh lemon juice
2 cloves garlic
Salt and pepper
¼ cup chopped fresh dill

In a medium saucepan, heat oil over medium-high heat. Cook onion and mushrooms until onion is soft and mushrooms begin to brown, about 6 minutes. Add green beans and 5 cups stock and bring to a boil. Cook, uncovered, about 10 minutes. Meanwhile, in a blender or food processor, combine and purée remaining stock with 1 cup of the chick peas, lemon juice, and garlic. Add to soup with remaining cup chick peas and cook another 5 minutes. Taste for salt and pepper and stir in dill just before serving.

Serves 6

SPICY TOMATO SOUP WITH DRIED JACK TORTILLA STRIPS

This soup appeals particularly to those fixated in the Cracker Jack stage—and who isn't? There's something about discovering the hidden treasure of tortilla strips, slathered with melted cheese, that brings back that old sense of surprise: Will there be one more down there? Did I already snare the last one? Even latter-day kids like to dig into this Mexican-inspired soup, although you might have to tone down the jalapeños for some.

2 tablespoons butter or oil
¼ cup chopped shallots
2 cloves garlic, chopped
2 jalapeño peppers, seeded and chopped
1 teaspoon ground coriander
¼ cup chopped fresh cilantro leaves
½ teaspoon dried oregano
3 pounds tomatoes, seeded and chopped
1 tablespoon tomato paste
1 tablespoon honey

4 cups Chicken Stock (page 20) or Vegetable
   Stock (page 25)
Salt and pepper

TORTILLA STRIPS
4 large (8-inch) flour tortillas
1 cup grated jack cheese

In a heavy medium nonreactive saucepan, heat oil over medium-high heat. Cook shallots, garlic, and jalapeños until soft, about 6 minutes. Stir in remaining ingredients except stock and simmer 10 minutes. Add stock and bring to a boil. Reduce heat and simmer, uncovered, 10 minutes. For a smoother soup, pass through a food mill. Season to taste with salt and pepper.

To make the tortilla strips, preheat the oven to 400 degrees F. Place tortillas on a baking sheet and sprinkle each with ¼ cup cheese. Bake until cheese is melted, about 5 minutes. When cooled, cut into 1½-inch strips with a pastry wheel.

Place about 4 tortilla strips in bottom of each soup bowl and ladle soup over them.

Serves 6

The directions here specify that the flour be cooked until it is "lightly browned." That is certainly the safest and most sensible way and one that will not endanger the end results. But some day, if you're feeling particularly daring, you might try cooking the flour until it's almost burned. (The key word here is "almost," and there's no telling how long that takes.) This is one of those Old World kitchen techniques that nobody writes down or even mentions unless somebody happens to ask. The resulting burnt roux produces a soup with tiny brown flecks and a nutty, fabulous flavor, and the fresh dill makes this a bright, tingly beginning to any meal.

¼ pound bacon, chopped
1 onion, chopped
4 tablespoons flour
2 medium tomatoes, seeded and coarsely chopped
3 tablespoons chopped fresh dill
6 cups Chicken Stock (page 20) or
  Beef Stock (page 21)
3 large potatoes, peeled and diced
Salt and pepper

In a heavy medium nonreactive saucepan, cook bacon and onions over medium heat until soft, about 5 minutes. Stir in flour and cook until flour is lightly browned, about 4 minutes. Stir in tomatoes and dill and cook about 3 minutes. Whisk in stock, about 1 cup at a time, making sure there are no lumps. Add potatoes and bring to a boil. Reduce heat and simmer, covered, 20 minutes. Taste for salt and pepper and serve.

Serves 6

MUSHROOM, SPINACH, AND RICE SOUP

Mark Twain might have called this soup a "stretcher." That was his word for exaggerating, or broadening, the truth a bit, or, well, lying. You won't find any lies in our soup, but you will see a lot of cultivated mushrooms browning up beautifully with a small number of shiitakes. This little mingle helps to stretch the flavors of the more costly shiitakes and infuse the soup with their rich earthiness. As a special first course, it alerts the palate that what follows will be no ordinary meal; it will be—as Twain would have called it—an "adventure."

---

3 tablespoons butter or oil

1 medium onion, chopped

1½ pounds fresh button mushrooms, coarsely chopped

½ pound fresh shiitake mushrooms, stems discarded, caps coarsely chopped

1 sprig fresh tarragon or ½ teaspoon dried tarragon

3 tablespoons balsamic vinegar

½ cup dry-packed sundried tomatoes, cut into strips

½ cup Arborio rice

6 cups coarsely chopped fresh spinach leaves

6 cups Mushroom Stock (page 26) or Vegetable Stock (page 25)

Salt and pepper

In a heavy medium nonreactive saucepan, heat butter over medium heat. Cook onion and mushrooms until onion is soft and mushrooms are slightly brown around edges, about 8 minutes. Stir in tarragon, vinegar, and tomatoes and cook until bubbly, about 2 minutes. Stir in rice and spinach and cook another 2 minutes. Add stock and bring to a boil. Reduce heat and simmer, uncovered, until rice is tender, about 20 minutes. Taste for salt and pepper.

Serves 6 to 8

Except for the giant California wild mushroom of Jurassic dimensions—measuring three feet across the cap and weighing up to four pounds—portobello mushrooms are about the largest one is likely to see, especially in the neighborhood supermarket. Cut in long, luxurious slivers, they make a dramatic and provocative addition to this starter.

---

2 tablespoons butter or oil
4 large portobello mushroom caps, cut into
*   thin strips*
1 leek, white part only, thoroughly washed
*   and sliced*
1 medium butternut squash, peeled, seeded,
*   and cut into 1-inch cubes*
½ teaspoon dried thyme
5 cups Chicken Stock (page 20)
½ cup heavy cream or half-and-half
Salt and pepper
¼ cup chopped chives

In a medium saucepan, heat butter over medium heat. Cook mushrooms over high heat until brown and dry, about 8 minutes. Remove and set aside.

Add leeks, squash, thyme, and stock to the same pan. Bring to a boil, reduce heat, and simmer until squash is tender, about 30 minutes. Purée mixture with cream in a food processor or blender. Taste for salt and pepper. Stir in reserved mushrooms and heat through if necessary. Sprinkle with chives and serve.

Serves 8

SUMMER SQUASH, POTATO, AND TOMATO SOUP

What makes this soup summer is everything in it—the sweet, ripe tomatoes, the colorful rounds of squash in summery yellow and green—but what turns it into a little ceremony is the basil tossed in at the last minute.

---

2 tablespoons olive oil
2 leeks, white parts only, thoroughly washed and thinly sliced
2 cloves garlic, minced
2 medium-size ripe tomatoes, seeded and cut into 1-inch chunks
2 zucchini, halved lengthwise and sliced ¼ inch thick

2 yellow summer squash, halved lengthwise and sliced ¼ inch thick
5 cups water
2 medium-size red new potatoes, cut into 1-inch chunks
¼ cup fresh basil leaves, cut into shreds
Salt and pepper

In a medium nonreactive saucepan, heat oil over medium-high heat. Cook leeks until soft, about 8 minutes. Stir in garlic and tomatoes. Cook over medium-high heat until bubbly, about 2 minutes. Add the zucchini and summer squash, stirring to coat with tomato mixture. Add water, bring to a boil, and add potatoes. Simmer, partly covered, 20 minutes. Ladle about 2 cups of soup into a food processor or blender. Purée and return the mixture to remaining soup in pot. Stir in basil. Taste for salt and pepper and serve.

Serves 6 to 8

When you're planning a substantial meal, this soup is just what you want a starter to be: a pretty and light prelude to almost any kind of entree, with just enough intrigue to set the taste buds wondering. The mix of winter and summer squashes makes it doable any time of the year.

---

2 tablespoons butter or oil
1 onion, chopped
2 cups winter squash, such as butternut,
  pumpkin, and acorn, peeled, seeded, and diced
1 potato, peeled and diced
6 cups Chicken Stock (page 20) or Vegetable
  Stock (page 25)
1 pound zucchini, chopped
Salt and pepper
¼ cup chopped fresh parsley
¼ cup chopped fresh basil

In a heavy medium saucepan, heat butter over medium heat. Cook onion until soft, about 5 minutes. Add winter squash, potato, and stock and bring to a boil. Reduce heat and simmer 20 minutes. Purée and return to pan. Stir in zucchini and cook another 5 minutes. Taste for salt and pepper. Sprinkle with parsley and basil and serve.

Serves 8

FENNEL, POTATO, AND GARLIC SOUP

"One-eyed bouillabaisse" is the fishless Provençal soup that inspired this fragrant first course. The intriguingly named soup—*aigo-sau-d'iou* in Provençal—translates as "soup without an eye," though no one seems to know what that means. Also called *bouillabaisse borgne,* it is a rich-tasting mix of potato, fennel, tomato, and garlic. We have used more garlic than usual, its flavor mellowed by the preliminary roasting.

---

12 cloves garlic, unpeeled
4 tablespoons olive oil
1 leek, white part only, thoroughly washed
  and thinly sliced
2 medium tomatoes, seeded and coarsely
  chopped
½ teaspoon herbes de Provence
2 medium fennel bulbs, trimmed, cored, and
  thinly sliced
3 large baking potatoes, peeled and cut into
  1-inch cubes
6 cups water
Salt and pepper

To roast the garlic, preheat the oven to 375 degrees F. Place garlic cloves in small ovenproof dish, drizzle with 1 tablespoon of the olive oil, and roast until cloves feel very soft, about 40 minutes. Set aside to cool, then remove peel from garlic.

In a large heavy nonreactive saucepan, heat the remaining oil over medium-high heat. Cook leek until soft, about 6 minutes. Stir in tomatoes and *herbes de Provence.* Bring to a boil and add peeled roasted garlic cloves and fennel. Add potatoes and the water and simmer, partly covered, 30 minutes. Taste for salt and pepper and serve.

Serves 6 to 8

To be honest, the pairing of fennel and parsnips has struck more than one outspoken dinner guest as somewhat peculiar. And yet licoricelike fennel makes a delicious contrast to the muted sweetness of parsnips. Such classics as Swedish *limpa,* a fennel bread flecked with orange, make good use of this licorice-sweet combination, as does the Italian custom of stuffing roasted figs with fennel and almonds. This fragrant starter soup gets its soft jade color from the feathery fennel greens added to the purée.

---

2 tablespoons butter or oil
1 medium onion, chopped
1 tablespoon crushed fennel seed
2 large fennel bulbs, trimmed, cored, and
  sliced (save feathery stalks for garnish)
2 parsnips, peeled and sliced
3 cups Vegetable Stock (page 25) or Chicken
  Stock (page 20)
Salt and pepper

In a heavy medium saucepan, heat butter over medium heat. Cook onion until soft, about 5 minutes. Stir in fennel seed. Add sliced fennel, parsnips, and stock. Cover and bring to a boil. Reduce heat and simmer until vegetables are very soft, about 30 minutes. Purée in a food processor with some reserved fennel greens. Taste for salt and pepper and serve garnished with chopped greens.

Serves 6

CELERY AND WATERCRESS SOUP WITH ROQUEFORT

This soup always reminds us of the Roquefort Man. In restaurant circles, he was known as the man with an extremely sharp tongue. He was employed by the Roquefort people to taste everything on a restaurant menu that mentioned Roquefort as an ingredient. If his sharp tongue ascertained that the dish was made with a blue-veined cheese other than Roquefort, he advised the establishment that they could not use the word Roquefort in their description. In this soup, you may substitute some other blue-veined cheese for the Roquefort; only the Roquefort Man will know for sure.

2 tablespoons butter
2 tablespoons chopped shallots
6 stalks celery, with leaves, chopped
½ teaspoon celery seed
½ teaspoon dried marjoram
4 cups Chicken Stock (page 20)
1 small potato, peeled and diced
1 bunch (6 ounces) watercress, leaves only
½ cup heavy cream
Salt and pepper
2 ounces Roquefort cheese
6 slices baguette, toasted

In a large heavy pot, heat butter over medium-high heat. Cook shallots and celery until soft, about 5 minutes. Stir in celery seed and marjoram. Cook another minute. Add stock and potato. Bring to a boil and simmer 20 minutes. Purée with watercress and ¼ cup of the cream. Taste for salt and pepper.

Combine Roquefort with remaining ¼ cup cream and spread on toasts. Reheat soup if necessary. Ladle into bowls, top each serving with a Roquefort toast, and serve.

Serves 6

Though everyone has heard of borscht, there is a relatively unknown soup that is considered the national soup of Russia. Called *shchi,* it is popular with Russians of all social classes and has been around for a thousand years. In its purest form, *shchi* begins with sauerkraut. Our version, based on a variation known as "lazy man's *shchi*" (in Russian, *Rakhmanovskie*), begins with cabbage, the one year-round staple of the Russian table. It is a harvest of autumn vegetables, which don't require the long cooking of the classic.

---

2 tablespoons olive oil

1 leek, white part only, thoroughly washed
    and thinly sliced

1 fennel bulb, trimmed and thinly sliced

½ pound mushrooms, sliced

½ small head green cabbage, shredded

2 tablespoons chopped fresh dill

4 tablespoons chopped fresh parsley

1 sweet potato, peeled and cut into 1-inch cubes

1 parsnip, peeled and sliced

3 cups diced and peeled winter squash,
    such as butternut, acorn, Delicata,
    Buttercup

6 cups Vegetable Stock (page 25) or Chicken
    Stock (page 20)

2 cups coarsely chopped broccoli

¼ pound spinach linguine, broken into 2-inch
    lengths

Salt and pepper

In a medium saucepan, heat oil over medium-high heat. Cook leek, fennel, mushrooms, and cabbage until wilted, about 7 minutes. Stir in dill, parsley, sweet potato, parsnip, winter squash, and stock and bring to a boil. Reduce heat and simmer 20 minutes. Add broccoli and linguine and cook another 10 minutes. Taste for salt and pepper and serve.

Serves 8

SPRING VEGETABLE SOUP

Although this soup is teeming with vegetables, its distinctive peppery nature comes from none of them. In fact, it's only after the soup is puréed with the watercress that its true springlike personality emerges. As a soup ingredient, the pungent streamside herb enjoys international fame from the French *velouté cressonnière* and *potage de santé* (a sophisticated health food soup) to an old Yankee dish, known simply as Vermont spring soup.

---

2 tablespoons vegetable oil
3 scallions, trimmed and sliced
2 cloves garlic, thinly sliced
2 small turnips, peeled and diced
2 new potatoes, scrubbed and diced
2 carrots, diced
1 sprig fresh thyme or ½ teaspoon dried thyme
½ cup chopped fresh parsley
6 cups Vegetable Stock (page 25) or Chicken
  Stock (page 20)
½ pound asparagus, trimmed and cut into
  1-inch pieces
1 cup peas, fresh or frozen
1 bunch (6 ounces) watercress, leaves only
2 tablespoons tarragon vinegar
Salt and pepper

In a medium saucepan, heat oil over medium-high heat. Add scallions, garlic, turnips, potatoes, and carrots. Cover and cook until vegetables are starting to soften, about 5 minutes. Stir in thyme, parsley, and stock and bring to a boil. Reduce heat and simmer 15 minutes. Add asparagus and peas and cook another 5 minutes. Purée half the soup with watercress and return it to remainder of soup. Stir in tarragon vinegar, taste for salt and pepper, and serve.

Serves 8

GRILLED SUMMER VEGETABLE SOUP WITH PESTO CREAM

The appetite-provoking aroma of grilled vegetables precedes this soup to the table and lingers long after the last soup bowl has been spooned dry. In fact, we should warn that it is not the best soup to serve as a starter because everybody always wants more. Made almost entirely on the outdoor grill, this soup is a good way to launch a barbecue. Alternatively, the vegetables may be roasted in an oven at 400 degrees F until soft, about 40 minutes.

1 head garlic
Olive oil
2 medium zucchini, halved lengthwise
1 medium eggplant, sliced ½ inch thick
1 large red bell pepper, quartered lengthwise
  and seeded
1 medium fennel bulb, core removed and
  quartered
2 leeks, white parts only, thoroughly washed
  and halved lengthwise

4 plum (Roma) tomatoes, halved lengthwise
6 cups Chicken Stock (page 20) or Vegetable
  Stock (page 25)
6 slices baguette
Salt and pepper

PESTO CREAM
½ cup Pesto (page 267)
½ cup crème fraîche, sour cream, or
  plain yogurt

Heat the grill until hot. Cut about ¼ inch from top of garlic head, exposing cloves. Brush entire head with olive oil and wrap in foil. Brush surfaces of remaining vegetables with oil. Place wrapped garlic and vegetables on grill. Grill vegetables until brown char marks appear and vegetables are soft, 3 to 4 minutes per side. Allow about 30 minutes for garlic.

Cut vegetables into bite-size pieces and place in a large saucepan. Remove garlic from foil and squeeze out cloves into saucepan. Add stock and simmer over medium heat about 10 minutes. Meanwhile, brush bread with olive oil and place on grill. Cook on both sides until toasted.

Combine pesto and cream and spread on toasts. Taste soup for salt and pepper. Place pesto cream toasts in soup bowls, ladle soup over them, and serve.

Serves 6

NOTES

dinner in a

bowl

We often refer to these soups as comfort soups, not only because hungry eaters like their homey, nourishing, mmm'mmm good qualities, but also because they comfort the cook! Once you select a recipe from this chapter, you can rest assured that, in one fell swoop, you've organized an entire meal. Each of these full-fledged dishes makes a satisfying, well-rounded entree and, as far as we know, none has ever elicited that "Is-this-all?" look, even from the most voracious adolescent. (If all else fails, try the Ballpark Soup!)

Combinations are fresh and sparkling and include everything from mussels to smoked duck sausages, from creamy white beans to summer corn. And many contain such unexpected surprises as dumplings or ravioli or a crispy crust of phyllo.

This fish-stocked minestrone may seem unorthodox, but we have uncovered many Italian vegetable soups enriched with seafood. A Venetian version for example, with the intriguing name *minestra alla cappuccina*, is made with fresh anchovies. Certainly our interpretation fits André Simon's definition of minestrone in *A Concise Encyclopedia of Gastronomy:* "A meal in itself." Our finale sprinkling of gremolata adds more than an afterthought. A pinch of this versatile parsley-lemon mixture, which may be made ahead and stored in the refrigerator for a week or so, can imbue any simple soup with a lively and elegant sparkle.

2 tablespoons olive oil
1 leek, white part only, thoroughly washed
  and thinly sliced
1 onion, chopped
1 small fennel bulb, trimmed, cored, and
  thinly sliced
1 large carrot, sliced
1 celery stalk, sliced
1 medium red bell pepper, seeded and
  thinly sliced
½ head savoy cabbage, cored and
  coarsely shredded
1 zucchini, sliced
½ teaspoon dried oregano
½ teaspoon dried thyme
1 cup coarsely chopped tomatoes
½ cup dry white wine

2 cups Fish Stock (page 24) or Vegetable
  Stock (page 25)
4 cups water
1 cup small pasta shells
½ pound medium shrimp, shelled and
  deveined
½ pound sea scallops, quartered
½ pound snapper, cut into chunks
½ pound sea bass or halibut, cut into chunks
Salt and pepper

GREMOLATA
1 bunch fresh parsley, leaves only
Zest of 1 small lemon
3 cloves garlic
2 ounces (⅔ cup) grated parmesan cheese

In a large heavy nonreactive pot, heat oil over medium-high heat. Sauté the vegetables until slightly softened, about 4 minutes. Stir in the oregano and thyme and cook another minute. Add tomatoes and wine and cook until bubbly, about 3 minutes. Add stock and water and bring to a boil. Add pasta and cook 12 minutes, stirring occasionally. Add fish and simmer about 3 minutes. Do not boil. Taste for salt and pepper.

To make the gremolata, process ingredients in a blender or food processor until they become a paste. Serve soup sprinkled with about 2 tablespoons of gremolata over each portion.

Serves 8 to 10

POTATO, TOMATO, AND RED SNAPPER SOUP

Although there are no clams in it, this soup gives you that old, chowdery feeling. Not that chowders must have clams. "Cod and bass make the best chowder," decreed Mrs. A. L. Webster in her *The Improved Housewife* (1842). She considered clams, at best, tolerable. Mary Lincoln, author of *The Boston School Kitchen Textbook* (1896) couldn't have agreed more. "A chowder is a stew of fish," she insisted. Whatever you call it, we like this soup on days when the leaves on the lawn are crisping up orange, and the sea air, real or remembered, rattles the windowpanes, and you feel like being caring and cared for.

1½ pounds red snapper fillets,
   small bones removed
3 tablespoons Pernod
1 tablespoon fresh tarragon leaves
   or 1 teaspoon dried tarragon
3 tablespoons olive oil
2 leeks, white parts only, thoroughly
   washed and chopped
1 clove garlic, minced
¼ cup sundried tomatoes, dry or
   oil packed, cut into strips
½ teaspoon crushed red pepper
½ teaspoon dried thyme
2 cups coarsely chopped tomatoes,
   fresh or canned with juice
½ cup dry white wine
3 cups Fish Stock (page 24) or clam juice
3 cups water
2 pounds potatoes, peeled and
   cut into 1½-inch cubes
½ cup milk or cream
Salt and pepper
¼ cup chopped chives

Blot snapper dry with a paper towel and sprinkle with Pernod and tarragon on each side. Let stand at room temperature about 15 minutes.

In a large heavy nonreactive pot, heat oil over medium-high heat. Cut snapper into 2-inch chunks and cook just until opaque, about 1½ minutes. Remove and set aside. In the same pot, cook leeks and garlic until soft, about 6 minutes. Stir in sundried tomatoes, pepper, thyme, chopped tomatoes, and wine. Cook until mixture thickens slightly, about 10 minutes.

Add stock and the water and bring to a boil. Add potatoes and cook until tender, about 13 minutes. Remove about 1 cup of mixture to a food processor or blender and purée with milk. Return mixture to pot and taste for salt and pepper. Return snapper to soup and heat through over medium heat. Sprinkle with chives and serve.

Serves 8

GINGERED FISH, MUSHROOM, AND SPINACH SOUP

This is a fantastic dish—light, spicy, and satisfying. "Seductive," one friend called it, citing the gorgeous, deep flavor of mushrooms offset by the pungency of fresh ginger. This is also the dish for any extreme health nuts on your guest list. They would probably know of the great benefits now credited to ginger: from curing colds to burning up calories and revving up the metabolism, thus making it possible to eat even more.

1 ounce dried Chinese black mushrooms,
*   soaked in 1 cup hot water 30 minutes*
1 tablespoon vegetable oil
1 tablespoon sesame oil
3 scallions, trimmed and chopped
2 cloves garlic, minced
2 tablespoons grated fresh ginger
6 cups Chicken Stock (page 20)
1 cup Fish Stock (page 24) or clam juice

1 tablespoon sherry vinegar
2 tablespoons low-sodium soy sauce
1½ pounds white fish fillets, such as halibut,
*   sea bass, roughy, snapper, cut into*
*   1-inch cubes*
½ pound spinach, coarsely chopped (about
*   8 cups)*
Salt and pepper

Drain mushrooms and reserve soaking liquid. Squeeze out excess liquid from mushrooms, discard stems, and cut caps into thin strips.

In a large heavy pot, heat vegetable and sesame oils over medium-high heat. Cook scallions, garlic, and ginger until soft, about 3 minutes. Add mushrooms and cook another 3 minutes.

Add chicken stock, fish stock, ½ cup of mushroom soaking liquid, vinegar, and soy sauce. Bring to a boil, reduce heat, and simmer about 5 minutes. Add fish and spinach and simmer another 4 minutes. Taste for salt and pepper and serve.

Serves 8

Adding Pernod is a favorite Gallic trick with fish soups, such as *bouillabaisse à la Coran d'Ys*, a classic in some of the little French coastal towns. This saffronless offering, with its plump pearls of orzo, has more in common with the densely noodled fish soups of Normandy.

1½ pounds halibut or sea bass, cut into
  1-inch chunks
3 tablespoons Pernod
2 tablespoons olive oil
1 large onion, thinly sliced
2 cloves garlic, minced
1 red or green bell pepper, seeded and sliced
1 teaspoon dried oregano
½ teaspoon crushed red pepper flakes
1 can (28 ounces) tomatoes, coarsely chopped
½ cup white wine
4 cups Fish Stock (page 24)
1 cup orzo
1 pound mussels, scrubbed
Salt and pepper

In a medium bowl, sprinkle fish with Pernod. Let marinate while preparing rest of soup.

In a large heavy nonreactive saucepan, heat oil over medium-high heat. Cook onion, garlic, and pepper until soft, about 5 minutes. Add oregano, red pepper flakes, and tomatoes. Bring to a boil and simmer about 10 minutes. Purée mixture with wine in a food processor or blender and return to saucepan. Stir in stock and bring to a boil. Add orzo and simmer 10 minutes. Add the halibut and mussels, cover, and simmer until mussels open, about 4 minutes. Discard any mussels that have not opened. Taste for salt and pepper and serve.

Serves 6

This soup reminds us of a day in Guadalajara or thereabouts, where jalapeños and cilantro are part of the natural wonders, along with sun-warmed tomatoes and the native corn called *elote*. In fact, Diana Kennedy discovered a Mexican shrimp soup named *guatape,* a specialty of Tampico, spiked with pulverized leaves called *hoja santa,* or holy leaf. Thick with sweet corn, this creamy shrimp soup can practically be a whole summer menu in itself.

---

3 tablespoons vegetable oil
¾ pound medium shrimp, shelled and deveined
6 scallions, trimmed and chopped
2 cloves garlic, minced
1 or 2 jalapeño peppers, seeded and chopped
½ teaspoon dried oregano
2 plum (Roma) tomatoes, seeded and chopped
4 cups corn kernels, fresh or frozen
1 cup milk
6 cups Chicken Stock (page 20) or Vegetable
    Stock (page 25)
Salt and pepper
¼ cup chopped cilantro

In a large heavy nonreactive pot, heat oil over medium-high heat. Cook shrimp just until they turn pink, about 2 minutes. Remove and set aside. Cook the scallions, garlic, and jalapeños in the same pot until soft. Stir in oregano and tomatoes and cook about 2 minutes. Purée 1 cup corn with milk and add to pot with remaining corn and stock. Bring to a boil, reduce heat, and simmer 10 minutes. Taste for salt and pepper. Return shrimp to soup and heat through. Garnish with cilantro and serve.

Serves 8

SHRIMP AND THREE ONION SOUP

This pearl-pink soup conveys the elegance and color of fresh shrimp. It has a lovely blend of flavors—a hint of licorice from tarragon and Pernod, the sweetness of lightly caramelized leeks and onions—that makes it almost irresistible.

---

3 tablespoons butter or vegetable oil
3 cloves garlic, minced
½ pound medium shrimp, shelled and deveined
¼ cup Pernod
2 leeks, white parts only, thoroughly washed
*   and chopped*
1 onion, chopped
¼ cup chopped shallots

1 teaspoon fresh tarragon or ½ teaspoon
*   dried tarragon*
2 tablespoons tomato paste
2 tablespoons flour
2 cups milk
3 cups Fish Stock (page 24) or water
Salt and pepper

In a medium saucepan, heat butter over medium heat. Add garlic and shrimp and cook just until prawns begin to turn pink. Remove and set aside. Add Pernod and cook until reduced to about 1 tablespoon. Pour over reserved shrimp.

Add leeks, onion, and shallots to the pan and cook until soft, about 5 minutes. Stir in tarragon and tomato paste. Cook for 1 minute. Stir in flour and cook, until dissolved, about 3 minutes. Pour in milk and cook until mixture thickens, about 3 minutes.

Purée in a blender or food processor and return to pot. Add stock or water and heat through, stirring until well blended. Taste for salt and pepper and add reserved prawns and juices that may have accumulated. Simmer another 2 minutes. Do not boil.

Serves 6

WEST COAST SHRIMP CHOWDER

The first chowder recipe published in this country appeared in 1751 in the *Boston Evening Post*. It was written like a poem: "Next lay some Fish cut crossways very nice/Then season well with Pepper, Salt and Spice . . . " That form seems appropriate for a dish with such homey and comforting associations. Derived from the French word *chaudière,* meaning stew pot, chowder recalls a time of iron cauldrons hung over the hearth, a world of slow simmering and crackling fires. Our postmodern interpretation bristles with West Coast sass: the audacity of artichokes, the blatant sun-worship of citrus, and that devil-may-care cilantro. It's chowder with an attitude, one that's both western and wise.

1 pound medium shrimp, shelled and deveined, cut into small pieces
¼ cup fresh lime juice
¼ cup fresh orange juice
1 dried chili pepper
¼ pound bacon, diced
6 scallions, trimmed and sliced
1 red bell pepper, seeded and chopped
2 cloves garlic, minced
1 pound red new potatoes, scrubbed and diced

1 zucchini, diced
1 cup artichoke hearts, fresh or frozen, quartered
1 bay leaf
½ teaspoon dried thyme
3 cups water
3 cups Fish Stock (page 24)
1 cup half-and-half or milk
Salt and pepper
¼ cup chopped fresh cilantro

In a medium nonreactive bowl, toss shrimp with lime juice, orange juice, and pepper. Let stand at room temperature 1 hour, tossing every so often.

In a large heavy pot, cook bacon until golden brown but not crisp. Remove all but 3 tablespoons bacon fat from pot. Add scallions, bell pepper, and garlic and cook until soft, about 6 minutes. Add potatoes, zucchini, artichoke hearts, bay leaf, thyme, the water, and stock. Bring to a boil, reduce heat, and simmer 20 minutes. Drain shrimp and add to soup. Simmer another 5 minutes. Stir in milk and taste for salt and pepper. Sprinkle with cilantro and serve.

Serves 8

TARRAGON SHRIMP AND ASPARAGUS SOUP

Whatever the recipe, asparagus soup is one of the most difficult to make. Our first important exposure, called *soupe tourangelle aux asperges,* was a creamed soup, originating in Touraine (hence *tourangelle*) and made popular by Simone Beck in her cookbook *Simca's Cuisine.* The difficulty in making asparagus soup lies not in the technique but in the decision to convert the voluptuously tactile stalks into a homogenous purée. To be honest, the only time we are able to do this without remorse is when we make this delicious soup.

3 tablespoons butter or vegetable oil
1 pound medium shrimp, shelled and deveined
2 pounds asparagus, trimmed, peeled, and cut
   into 2-inch pieces
¼ cup chopped shallots
2 teaspoons fresh tarragon leaves or 1 teaspoon
   dried tarragon
½ cup white wine
½ cup heavy cream
5 cups Chicken Stock (page 20)
Salt and pepper

In a large heavy pot, heat butter over medium heat. Sauté shrimp just until they turn pink, about 3 minutes. Remove and set aside. Add asparagus to the same pot, cover, and cook until tender, about 5 minutes. Remove and set aside. Stir in shallots, tarragon, and wine and cook until shallots are soft and wine is reduced to about ¼ cup, about 6 minutes. Purée cream with about a third of the asparagus in a food processor or blender and add to pot along with chicken stock. Bring to a boil, reduce heat, and simmer. Return remaining asparagus and shrimp to pot and cook 3 minutes. Taste for salt and pepper and serve.

Serves 6

Anyone who visits the French seacoast town of La Rochelle learns one new word: *mouclade*. This classic mussel creation, with its golden shimmer from a touch of curry, seems to capture the essence of the picturesque sun-slathered port, where mussel farms line the coast. Since most mussels now come from mussel farms in our country as well, you can serve this *mouclade*-inspired soup year-round.

¼ cup chopped shallots
2 tablespoons chopped fresh parsley
½ stalk celery, chopped
1 bay leaf
1 teaspoon fresh thyme or ½ teaspoon
  dried thyme
¾ cup white wine
3 pounds mussels, scrubbed
2 tablespoons olive oil

1 small onion, chopped
1 small tomato, chopped
4 medium carrots, chopped
2 tablespoons flour
¼ teaspoon cayenne
2 cups Fish Stock (page 24)
½ cup heavy cream
Salt and pepper
¼ cup fresh chervil

In a large heavy pot, combine shallots, parsley, celery, bay leaf, thyme, wine, and mussels. Cover and cook over medium-high heat, until mussels open, 3 to 5 minutes. Discard any that do not open. With a slotted spoon, remove mussels to a bowl and strain the liquid through a fine-mesh strainer. Set aside liquid. Shell mussels and discard shells. Set aside mussels.

In a large heavy nonreactive pot, heat oil over medium-high heat. Add onion and cook until soft, about 4 minutes. Stir in tomato, carrots, flour, and cayenne and cook 4 minutes. Add reserved mussel liquid and stock. Bring to a boil, reduce heat, and simmer about 20 minutes. Purée in a blender or food processor and return to pot. Stir in cream and taste for salt and pepper. Add shelled mussels and reheat over low heat about 3 minutes. Sprinkle with chervil and serve.

Serves 6

CLAM AND MUSHROOM CHOWDER

Clam chowder cook-offs have not become as prevalent—nor as notorious—as chili cook-offs, but their participants are no less obsessive about their favorite recipe. And chowderheads may even be worse than chiliheads on the essential (and insoluble) issues, such as Manhattan vs. New England. One of the country's more lighthearted competitions takes place every year along the boardwalk in Santa Cruz, California, somewhere between the merry-go-round and the Pacific Ocean. About 50 mostly amateur cooks, dressed as mermaids, scuba divers, clamanauts and, yes, Main-i-acs—they claim to be from Maine—dish out about 500 gallons of soup in Styrofoam cups. From our experience on the panel of official judges, we can report with confidence that our mushroomy mélange outchowders most of the competition. This is one of those pantry recipes that calls for canned clams so you can make it almost anytime. (Just don't serve it in Styrofoam cups.)

¼ pound bacon, diced
1 onion, chopped
1 stalk celery, sliced
1 small carrot, diced
1 pound mushrooms, sliced
1 cup chopped tomatoes
1 teaspoon fresh thyme or ½ teaspoon
  dried thyme

2 tablespoons flour
3 cups Fish Stock (page 24)
3 cups water
1 pound red potatoes, scrubbed and diced
1 can (10 ounces) baby clams
Salt and pepper
2 tablespoons chopped fresh dill
2 tablespoons chopped fresh parsley

In a large heavy nonreactive pot, cook bacon over medium-high heat until most of the fat is rendered. Remove all but 2 tablespoons of fat from pot. Add onion, celery, carrot, and mushrooms and cook until soft, about 6 minutes. Stir in tomatoes and thyme and cook until bubbly. Stir in flour and cook another 3 minutes. Add stock and the water and bring to a boil. Add potatoes and cook, covered, 15 minutes. Add clams and liquid from can and cook another 5 minutes. Taste for salt and pepper. Stir in dill and parsley and serve.

Serves 6

Although apple pie is usually cited as the most American thing in the world, pot pie goes back just as far. Chicken may now be the most common filling, but early versions were made with everything from passenger pigeons, squirrels, all sorts of game and domestic animals. For harvest celebrations and wedding feasts, mammoth pies were constructed, filled with no fewer than a dozen hens and roosters plus vegetables! These individual pies, with their flaky, melting covers of delicate phyllo leaves, seem more suited to today's postfrontier conditions.

2 tablespoons butter or oil
1 small onion, diced
2 stalks celery, sliced
6 large mushrooms, quartered
7 cups Chicken Stock (page 20)
12 baby carrots, peeled
6 small red new potatoes, scrubbed and
*   quartered*
½ pound green beans, cut into 1-inch pieces
1½ pounds skinless and boneless chicken
*   breast, cut into strips*
1 tablespoon chopped fresh dill
1 tablespoon chopped fresh parsley
Salt and pepper

PHYLLO CRUST
8 sheets phyllo dough, defrosted overnight in
*   the refrigerator*
½ cup melted butter or vegetable oil
2 tablespoons chopped fresh parsley
2 tablespoons chopped fresh dill

In a large saucepan, heat butter over medium heat. Cook onion, celery, and mushrooms until soft, about 5 minutes. Add stock, carrots, and potatoes and simmer 15 minutes. Add green beans and chicken and cook another 6 minutes. Stir in dill and parsley and taste for salt and pepper.

Preheat the oven to 375 degrees F. Ladle warm or hot soup into 6 ovenproof soup bowls. Place a sheet of phyllo dough on a clean surface. Brush sparingly with butter and sprinkle with some parsley and dill. Continue until you have a stack of 4 sheets of phyllo dough. Cut 3 circles 2 inches larger than diameter of the top of the soup bowl. Brush tops of phyllo circles with butter and invert circles on the soup bowls, buttered side down. Press edges of phyllo dough against bowls and brush tops with butter. With a sharp knife, cut 2 slits in each. Repeat with remaining phyllo dough and soup bowls. Place bowls on a baking sheet and bake until tops are golden brown and puffed, about 20 minutes. Serve immediately.

Serves 6

The very word dumplings makes a meal homey. Perhaps that's why they appear in so many of the world's cuisines in so many shapes and guises. Germany has its flour dumplings (*Mehlmusklösschen*) and marrow dumplings (*Markklösschen*) as well as its fiddle-peg dumplings (*Geigenknöpfle*) called *Münchnernockerln* in Bavaria, made from bread crumbs. The Czechs made dumpling craft a national pastime with their unprecedented range of ingredients from ground meat, potatoes, and bread to dessert dumplings fashioned around whole plums (*svestkove knedliky*). Ours are a bit on the French side, resembling light, diminutive quenelles. Guests love them, especially in this warming lentil soup.

DUMPLINGS

½ pound boneless and skinless chicken
   breast, cut up
2 tablespoons oil
½ small onion
½ cup fresh (not dried) bread crumbs
1 egg plus 1 egg white
1 tablespoon heavy cream
½ teaspoon salt
⅛ teaspoon cayenne
¼ teaspoon grated nutmeg

SOUP

2 tablespoons oil
1 large onion, thinly sliced
1 clove garlic, minced
½ pound chard
2 cups lentils
8 cups Chicken Stock (page 20) or Vegetable
   Stock (page 25)
Salt and pepper

To make the dumplings, combine all ingredients in a food processor or blender and process until puréed. Chill mixture about 1 hour. With wet hands, form into balls, using about 1 tablespoon of mixture for each. Drop into a large pot of boiling salted water. Reduce heat and simmer until dumplings float to surface, about 12 minutes. Remove with slotted spoon and set aside.

To make the soup, in a large pot, heat oil over medium-high heat and sauté onion and garlic until soft, about 5 minutes. Separate stems from leaves of chard and cut stems into 2-inch pieces. Add to onion and cook another 2 minutes. Stir in lentils and stock and bring to a boil. Simmer until lentils are tender, about 25 minutes. Cut chard leaves into thin strips and add to soup. Simmer 5 minutes. Purée in a food processor or blender about 1 cup of soup mixture and stir into remaining soup. Taste for salt and pepper. Place 4 or 5 dumplings in each soup plate, ladle soup over them, and serve.

Serves 8

Everything about couscous is exotic, starting with the word itself. Some say it is onomatopoeic, from steam whispering through the granules as they cook. The traditional North African process of preparing couscous—which this recipe does not require, we might add—begins with hand rubbing the granules, letting them dry for several hours, and then steaming them over broth in a special utensil called a *couscoussière*. Finally the couscous and some broth go into a pan covered with a wool blanket to swell as it absorbs the broth. One of couscous' most exotic and famous forms is *couscous au chameau* (Camel couscous). We are told in *Larousse Gastronomique* that "The hump, the feet and the stomach are the parts most appreciated by connoisseurs."

---

4 tablespoons vegetable oil
2 onions, chopped
4 cloves garlic, minced
1 red bell pepper, seeded and diced
2 teaspoons curry powder
1 teaspoon ground cumin
½ teaspoon turmeric
1 cup coarsely chopped tomatoes
2 carrots, sliced
1 small butternut squash, peeled, seeded, and
 cut into 1-inch cubes

1 parsnip, peeled and sliced
2 zucchini, sliced
1 cinnamon stick
10 cups Chicken Stock (page 20)
2 pounds boneless and skinless chicken
 breast, cut into strips
Salt and pepper
1 package (12 oz.) quick-cooking couscous,
 cooked according to package directions
¼ cup chopped fresh cilantro leaves

In a large heavy nonreactive pot, heat oil over medium-high heat. Sauté onions, garlic, and pepper until soft, about 5 minutes. Stir in curry, cumin, and turmeric and cook another minute. Add tomatoes and cook until bubbly. Stir in vegetables and cinnamon stick. Cook about 2 minutes. Add stock and bring to a boil. Reduce heat and simmer, partly covered, 15 minutes. Add chicken and simmer another 8 minutes.

Remove cinnamon stick from soup and taste for salt and pepper. Place cooked couscous in bowls, ladle soup over it, sprinkle with cilantro, and serve.

Serves 8

CHICKEN, FENNEL, AND ARTICHOKE SOUP

This soul-satisfying dish, so full of texture and flavor, contains just about every nutritional element that exists. It is also a thing of beauty, with its flecks of sundried tomato, chunks of tender chicken, and feathery fennel. A leafy salad and a crusty olive bread can turn this soup into an event.

---

2 boneless, skinless chicken breast halves, cut
*   into 1-inch cubes*
Salt and pepper
Flour for dredging
2 tablespoons olive oil
¼ cup chopped shallots
2 medium bulbs fennel, trimmed, quartered,
*   cored, and finely sliced, feathery stalks reserved*
12 artichoke hearts, fresh or frozen, quartered
¼ cup dry-pack sundried tomatoes, cut into
*   thin strips*
8 cups Chicken Stock (page 20)
1 cup cooked small white beans

Sprinkle the chicken with salt and pepper and lightly dredge in flour. In a medium saucepan, heat oil over medium-high heat. Cook chicken until golden on all sides. Remove and set aside. In the same pan, cook shallots and fennel until soft, about 8 minutes. Add artichoke hearts, tomatoes, and stock. Bring to a boil, reduce heat, and simmer, partly covered, 20 minutes. Return chicken to pot with beans and simmer another 5 minutes. Chop some of the fennel greens. Taste soup for salt and pepper, garnish with chopped greens, and serve.

Serves 8

To lie or not to lie, that is your dilemma when you serve this soup and someone asks you what it's called. Do you say the word succotash, thereby running the risk that your guests will look at you suspiciously. Actually everyone loves this thick, corn-sweet chowder, especially if you tell them something of its pedigree: that the American Indians made *msickquatash* and froze it in blocks so they could enjoy chunks of it all winter—defrosted, of course. The dish impressed the early colonists, who adopted it, adding their own regional variations. This is our soupified version.

---

2 tablespoons vegetable oil or butter

1 pound boneless and skinless chicken breast, cut into strips

¼ teaspoon cayenne

½ teaspoon salt

1 small onion, chopped

1 cup green peas, fresh or frozen

1 cup cooked lima beans

2 cups corn kernels, fresh or frozen

1 pound potatoes, peeled and diced

6 cups Chicken Stock (page 20)

½ teaspoon grated nutmeg

1 teaspoon fresh thyme or ½ teaspoon dried thyme

1 cup milk

Salt and pepper

3 tablespoons chopped fresh parsley

In a large heavy pot, heat the oil over medium-high heat. Cook chicken until golden brown and sprinkle with cayenne and salt. Remove and set aside. Cook onion in same pot until soft, about 4 minutes. Add peas, lima beans, 1 cup corn, potatoes, and stock. Bring to a boil and add nutmeg and thyme. Reduce heat and simmer, partly covered, 20 minutes. In a blender, purée remaining corn with milk and add to soup along with reserved chicken. Simmer another 5 minutes. Taste for salt and pepper, sprinkle with parsley, and serve.

Serves 6 to 8

TURKEY AND TURKEY SAUSAGE GUMBO

Like many modern-day gumbos, this crowded bowlful of goodies does not fully comply with some purists' requirements. It is thickened with a roux rather than the more exotic filé powder and the turkey sausage makes it a light, though richly spiced, interpretation. However, what people enjoy most is the surprising, peppery chunks of marinated turkey.

---

2 cloves garlic, minced
½ teaspoon salt
½ teaspoon cayenne
½ teaspoon hot pepper sauce
1 pound boneless, skinless turkey breast, cut into 1-inch cubes
1 pound spicy turkey sausage, sliced ¼ inch thick

3 tablespoons flour
3 tablespoons vegetable oil
1 small onion, chopped
4 scallions, trimmed and chopped
1 green bell pepper, seeded and chopped
2 stalks celery, chopped
8 cups Chicken Stock (page 20) or Turkey Stock

In a medium bowl, combine garlic, salt, cayenne, and hot pepper sauce. Add turkey pieces, toss to coat well, cover, and marinate about 1 hour.

In a small skillet, brown sausage slices over medium-high heat. Remove and set aside. Remove turkey pieces from marinade using a slotted spoon and dredge in 2 tablespoons of the flour. In a large heavy pot, heat oil and sauté turkey, stirring in marinade juices. Cook about 5 minutes. Remove turkey with a slotted spoon and set aside.

Add onion, scallions, bell pepper, and celery and cook until softened, about 5 minutes. Stir in remaining 1 tablespoon flour and cook until it darkens. Add a little stock and stir until smooth. Gradually add remaining stock and the sausage. Simmer about 10 minutes and add turkey. Simmer another 10 minutes.

Serves 8

"He who has not eaten" caponata, proclaimed Italian writer Gaetano Falzone, "has never reached the antechamber of the terrestrial paradise." Although we never thought of caponata in quite those terms, we definitely wanted to harness its lusty Sicilian charms into a soup. The word itself may come from the Latin *caupo,* meaning tavern, because it was served at inns and wayside places. Giuliano Bugialli, however, associates caponata with some ancient sweet-and-sour dishes called *cappone.* We hope this variation on a theme will provide a taste of Signor Falzone's paradise.

---

2 pounds leg of lamb, cut into 1-inch cubes
Salt and pepper
Flour for dredging
3 tablespoons olive oil
1 small onion, chopped
2 cloves garlic, minced
1 stalk celery, sliced
1 small red bell pepper, seeded and diced
3 Japanese eggplants, cut into 1-inch cubes
1 cup chopped tomatoes

2 tablespoons sugar dissolved in
  3 tablespoons red wine vinegar
½ cup imported green olives, pitted and
  halved
2 tablespoons capers, rinsed
7 cups Chicken Stock (page 20) or Beef
  Stock (page 21)
3 medium potatoes, peeled and cut into
  1-inch cubes
¼ cup chopped fresh parsley

Sprinkle lamb cubes with salt and pepper and dredge in flour, shaking off excess. In a large heavy nonreactive saucepan, heat oil over medium-high heat. Brown lamb on all sides, remove, and set aside. In same pan, cook onion, garlic, celery, pepper, and eggplant until slightly softened, about 8 minutes.

Stir in tomatoes, sugar mixture, olives, capers, reserved lamb, and stock. Simmer until lamb is almost tender, about 45 minutes. Add potatoes and simmer until tender, about 15 minutes. Taste for salt and pepper, sprinkle with parsley, and serve.

Serves 8

PROVENÇAL BEEF SOUP

When the word *Provençal* describes a dish, it sets off many hopes in the hungry eater: fresh tomatoes, garlic, olive oil, anchovies, and lots of capers. Despite their tiny size, these pungent little pearls have a great impact on taste and texture. And they have been enjoyed for a long time, judging from their appearance in the Gilgamesh epic, which was found inscribed on stone tablets dating from 2000 B.C. Although the capers are chopped with herbs and anchovies as a final blessing for this savory soup, aficionados will recognize the commanding presence of capers instantly.

---

2 tablespoons olive oil
2 pounds beef chuck, cut into 1-inch cubes
Salt and pepper
Flour for dredging
1 onion, chopped
3 cloves garlic, minced
1 red bell pepper, seeded and diced
½ teaspoon dried rosemary
½ teaspoon dried thyme
2 cups chopped tomatoes
2 tablespoons tomato paste

8 cups Beef Stock (page 21)
2 pounds small red, new potatoes, scrubbed
    and cut into 1-inch cubes

GARNISH
4 tablespoons chopped fresh parsley
1 tablespoon fresh oregano or 1 teaspoon
    dried oregano
1 clove garlic
2 tablespoon capers, rinsed
6 anchovy fillets

In a large heavy nonreactive pot, heat oil over medium-high heat. Sprinkle beef with salt and pepper and dredge lightly in flour. Brown beef on all sides. Remove and set aside. Add more oil if needed and cook onion, garlic, and pepper until soft, about 5 minutes. Stir in rosemary, thyme, tomatoes, and tomato paste. Cook until bubbly. Return beef to pot and stir to coat with sauce. Add stock and simmer 1 hour. Add potatoes and cook another 20 minutes.

To make the garnish, coarsely chop together parsley, oregano, garlic, capers, and anchovies. Sprinkle some of the mixture over each serving.

Serves 8

When it comes to child-pleasing cuisine, familiarity breeds acceptance. Kids like to know what they're eating *before* they're eating it. To a child, the name *is* the game. For example, kids are much more likely to eat meat loaf than *polpettone,* and potato soup sounds more edible than vichyssoise. So the next time you face the old double-dare-you question "What's for dinner?" try this soup. You may get no perceptible reaction, but you probably won't get any objections. Occasionally you may even be greeted with an enthusiastic "Yo, Mama!"

SOUP

3 tablespoons oil

½ cup chopped onion

2 cloves garlic, chopped

2 zucchini, diced

¼ cup sundried tomatoes, chopped

1 can (28 ounces) tomatoes, chopped

4 cups Chicken Stock (page 20) or Beef Stock (page 21)

4 ounces spaghetti, broken into 4-inch pieces

¼ cup fresh basil, cut into strips

Salt and pepper

½ cup grated Parmesan cheese (optional)

MEATBALLS

1 pound ground beef, turkey, chicken, lamb, or veal, or a mixture of two or more

2 tablespoons tomato paste

½ cup finely chopped onion

½ teaspoon dried oregano

¼ cup chopped fresh parsley

½ cup dried bread crumbs

¼ cup grated parmesan cheese

½ teaspoon salt

½ teaspoon ground pepper

To make meatballs, mix all ingredients together until well blended. Form into 12 or 16 balls. In a large heavy nonreactive pot, heat 2 tablespoons of the oil over medium-high heat. Cook meatballs until brown all over. Remove and set aside.

Add remaining tablespoon oil to pot. Cook onion, garlic, zucchini, and sundried tomatoes until soft, about 5 minutes. Add canned tomatoes and stock. Bring to a boil, reduce heat, and simmer 5 minutes. Add meatballs to soup and simmer gently 15 minutes. Add spaghetti and cook another 10 minutes. Stir in basil, taste for salt and pepper, and serve. Pass cheese separately.

Serves 6 to 8

WHITE BEAN AND RED CABBAGE SOUP WITH BEEF CUBES

There's something innately satisfying about "soaking" recipes. You feel, as you trundle off to bed with your beans safely submerged in an old pot, that you've already begun, that you're actually doing something even as you pull the blankets over sleep-drowsed eyelids. Something's going on, the water is working, all you have to do is finish things off later. With this soup, it's mostly true: a little chopping, slicing, and mincing and you have it—dinner for twelve, complete with a haunting flavor owed to the Tuscan pairing of white beans and sage.

2 cups white beans
3 tablespoons vegetable oil
1½ pounds beef stew meat, cut into
  1½-inch cubes
1 large onion, chopped
3 cloves garlic, minced
1 small head red cabbage, shredded
1 carrot, sliced ½ inch thick

1 stalk celery, sliced
1 parsnip, peeled and sliced
1 large baking potato, peeled and cubed
½ teaspoon rubbed sage
3 cups Beef Stock (page 21)
5 cups water
Salt and pepper
¼ cup chopped fresh dill

Soak beans in cold water to cover overnight. Drain the beans and set aside.

In a large heavy pot, heat oil over medium-high heat. Brown beef on all sides. Stir in onion and garlic and cook until soft, about 5 minutes. Add cabbage, carrot, celery, parsnip, potato, and sage. Cook about 2 minutes. Stir in beans, stock, and the water, bring to a boil, reduce heat, and simmer until beef is tender, about 1½ hours. Skim any fat that forms on surface. Taste for salt and pepper. Sprinkle with dill and serve.

Serves 10 to 12

RED CABBAGE, POTATO, AND KIELBASA SOUP

A rainy night, a CD full of Chopin, and a basketful of oven-warmed *razowy chleb* (pumpernickel bread) are all the accompaniments you'll need for this Polish dinner-in-a-bowl. A last-minute sprinkling of freshly grated horseradish (if you like) gives this sausage-spicy dish a final pungent kick.

1 pound kielbasa sausage, sliced ¼ inch thick
1 red onion, chopped
2 cloves garlic, minced
1 teaspoon dried rosemary
4 cups shredded red cabbage
1 cup chopped tomatoes
6 cups Chicken Stock (page 20) or Beef Stock
  (page 21)
2 medium potatoes, peeled and cut into
  ½-inch cubes
Salt and pepper

In a large heavy nonreactive pot, brown sausage on both sides over medium-high heat. Remove and set aside. Pour out all but 3 tablespoons fat and stir in onion, garlic, and rosemary. Cook until soft, about 5 minutes. Stir in cabbage and tomatoes. Simmer until cabbage is slightly wilted, about 3 minutes. Add stock, bring to a boil, and add potatoes. Reduce heat and simmer, partly covered, 20 minutes. Add sausage to soup and cook another 5 minutes. Taste for salt and pepper and serve.

Serves 8

SPINACH, WHITE BEAN, AND SPICY SAUSAGE SOUP

Just making this soup makes you feel healthy and stalwart and fit as a farm wife—or a farm husband, we add hastily, to avoid the dreaded accusation of gender bias. The homey mix begins with the sturdy knife work of chopping onions, parsley, and fresh spinach, slicing up squash and sausages. Even "grated" nutmeg and "crumbled" sage connote a sense of energy and vigor. And yet, with cooked beans, this dish takes only minutes to put together. A humble dish fit for a queen—or even, needless to say, her royal husband.

1 pound smoked spicy sausage, sliced ¼ inch thick
1 medium onion, chopped
2 cloves garlic, minced
½ teaspoon grated nutmeg
½ teaspoon crumbled dried sage
2 summer squash, sliced
1 pound fresh spinach, coarsely chopped
8 cups Chicken Stock (page 20) or Vegetable
  Stock (page 25)
2 cups cooked white beans
Salt and pepper
¼ cup chopped fresh parsley

In a large heavy pot, cook sausage over medium-high heat until lightly browned and most of the fat is rendered. Remove sausage and set aside. There should be about 2 to 3 tablespoons of fat remaining. In the same pot, cook onion until soft, about 5 minutes. Stir in garlic, nutmeg, sage, and summer squash and cook about 2 minutes. Add spinach and cook just until it begins to wilt, about 1 minute. Add stock, bring to a boil, and add beans. Reduce heat and simmer 10 minutes. Add sausage to soup and taste for salt and pepper. Sprinkle with parsley and serve.

Serves 8

WILD MUSHROOM, SWEET SAUSAGE, AND RICE SOUP

This delicious Italianate soup, with wild mushrooms, gets its nubby bite from Arborio rice. Originating in northern Italy in the valley lands around the Po River, the short-grained Arborio is the rice of risotto because it retains its shape as well as its moisture content when cooked. Italians, in their enviably colorful language, call this quality *al onde,* like the waves. Italians use Arborio rice for other less likely rice dishes, such as *gelato di riso,* an ice cream that gets its crunch from the cooked Arborio. Its toothy allure makes this soup a much-requested crowd-pleaser.

---

1 ounce (½ cup) dried porcini mushrooms
½ pound Italian sweet sausage, crumbled
1 small onion, chopped
½ pound fresh shiitake mushrooms, stems
  discarded, caps cut into thin strips
1 large ripe tomato, seeded and
  coarsely chopped

½ cup Arborio rice
6 cups Chicken Stock (page 20)
Salt and pepper
4 tablespoons chopped fresh basil

Soak porcini mushrooms in hot water 30 minutes. In a large heavy nonreactive saucepan, cook sausage, breaking up lumps, about 8 minutes. Remove to a strainer and set aside. Drain porcini mushrooms, reserving about ½ cup of the soaking water; then rinse away any clinging sand and chop coarsely.

Remove all but 2 tablespoons of fat from saucepan and stir in onion and soaked mushrooms and shiitakes. Cook until mushrooms begin to brown. Add tomato and rice and cook over medium heat 3 minutes. Add stock, bring to a boil, reduce heat, and simmer 15 minutes. Add sausage and reserved soaking water. Simmer another 5 minutes. Taste for salt and pepper. Garnish with basil and serve.

Serves 6 to 8

HAYDN'S TWO PEA SOUP WITH SMOKED DUCK SAUSAGE

On New Year's Day, 1791, Franz Joseph Haydn arrived in England for the first time. He was welcomed enthusiastically by his host who, we are told, "received him with open arms and good pea soup." Someone (not us) might call this variation on the pea soup theme a symphony of tastes: its harmony of fresh and dry, its subtle licoricelike undertone of chervil, the bold, smoky notes of duck sausage, all played against the unexpected gold tone of yellow peas, though you can certainly substitute the conventional green. In any case, we dedicate this soup to Haydn and to all out-of-town guests for whom you want to orchestrate a warm, hearty welcome.

---

1 pound smoked duck sausage, sliced
   ¼ inch thick
Vegetable oil
2 leeks, white parts only, thoroughly
   washed and chopped
2 cloves garlic, minced
2 carrots, chopped
1 stalk celery, chopped

2 tablespoons chopped fresh chervil
   or parsley
10 cups Chicken Stock (page 20) or
   Vegetable Stock (page 25)
1½ cups yellow split peas
2 cups peas, fresh or frozen
Salt and pepper
4 tablespoons chopped fresh mint

In a large heavy pot, brown sausage over medium-high heat until most of fat is rendered. Remove and set aside. Add more oil if needed and cook leeks, garlic, carrots, and celery until soft, about 8 minutes. Stir in chervil and stock. Bring to a boil and add split peas. Reduce heat and simmer, partly covered, about 1 hour. Purée half the soup in a food processor or blender. Return to pot with peas and reserved sausage. Simmer about 8 minutes. Taste for salt and pepper. Serve sprinkled with chopped mint.

Serves 10 to 12

Probably you have never licked your lips with glee over the prospect of eating a bunch of rutabagas or parsnips or anything else that qualifies as a winter root. But put together in this soup, these vegetables prove that the whole can taste better than the sum of its parts, especially under the dramatic influence of the chicken-apple sausage.

---

3 tablespoons olive oil
1 pound smoked chicken and apple sausage,
  cut in half lengthwise, and sliced
  ¼ inch thick
1 large onion, chopped
1 leek, white part only, thoroughly washed
  and chopped
½ teaspoon dried thyme
4 medium parsnips, peeled and diced
1 large rutabaga, peeled and diced
2 large carrots, diced
1 medium celery root, peeled and diced
6 cups Chicken Stock (page 20)
½ cup half-and-half
Salt and pepper

In a large heavy saucepan, heat oil over medium-high heat. Add sausage and brown on all sides. With a slotted spoon, remove sausage and set aside. Add onion and leek to saucepan and cook until soft, about 5 minutes. Stir in thyme, parsnips, rutabaga, carrots and celery root. Cook about 5 minutes, stirring occasionally. Add stock, bring to a boil, and reduce heat to a simmer. Cook until all vegetables are tender, about 30 minutes. Remove about 2 cups of soup mixture to a food processor or blender and purée with half-and-half. Return to pot and add reserved sausage. Heat through, taste for salt and pepper, and serve.

Serves 8

RED LENTIL, POTATO, AND LAMB SAUSAGE SOUP

Although lentils are standbys in many cuisines, for abundance and long-term allegiance no country surpasses India. Among the 60 or so varieties that have been cooked since Vedic times, colors range from black and white, to green, yellow, and brown. The reddish or pink lentils (*malika Masoor*) melt quickly into a butter-smooth purée. Indian cooks prepare lentils in myriad ways. For lentil soups, such as this Punjab-inspired mélange, the most revered method is the village way of cooking in ancient iron pots, sealed tightly and left to cook slowly near the fire on hot ashes.

½ pound lamb sausage, halved lengthwise
*   and sliced ¼ inch thick*

1 onion, chopped
2 cloves garlic, chopped
1 stalk celery, chopped
1 cup red lentils
1 cup chopped tomatoes
1 pound new potatoes, scrubbed and cut into
*   1-inch cubes*
6 cups water or Chicken Stock (page 20)
Salt and pepper
½ cup chopped fresh cilantro

SPICE MIXTURE
½ teaspoon ground turmeric
½ teaspoon ground cinnamon
1 teaspoon ground cumin
⅛ teaspoon cayenne
¼ teaspoon ground ginger

In a large heavy nonreactive pot, cook sausage until browned and most of fat is rendered. Remove sausage and set aside. You should have about 3 tablespoons fat in pot. In a small bowl, mix spices and add to pot with onion, garlic, celery, and lentils. Cook, stirring, until vegetables soften and spices become fragrant, about 6 minutes. Stir in tomatoes and cook until bubbly. Add potatoes and water and bring to a boil. Reduce heat and simmer 20 minutes. Purée about 2 cups of mixture in a blender or food processor and return to soup. Add reserved sausage. Heat through and taste for salt and pepper. Sprinkle with cilantro and serve.

Serves 8

A couple of cookbook authors we know grew up in Brooklyn when the Dodgers played where they belong—in Brooklyn! No self-respecting ballpark, especially Ebbets Field, ever served anything as elegant as a bowl of soup. A ballpark is a place for nutritional abandon. This souped-up version of bleacher cuisine appeals to fans of all ages, even if you substitute some of the newfangled hot dogs, such as those made from turkey, vegetables, or tofu. Should you happen to have a jar of mundane yellow mustard around, so much the better. We'd like to think of this soup as one of the joys of summer, but it is probably best at the end of the season—the baseball season, that is.

---

2 pounds hot dogs, sliced ½ inch thick
Vegetable oil
2 large onions, thinly sliced
1 small head green cabbage, cored and thinly
  shredded
2 tablespoons brown sugar
2 tablespoons red wine vinegar
1 tablespoon caraway seed

1 can (6 ounces) tomato paste
8 cups Beef Stock (page 21)
2 medium potatoes, peeled and cubed
2 cups cooked pinto beans
2 tablespoons yellow ballpark mustard
Salt and pepper

In a large heavy nonreactive pot, cook the hot dog slices over medium-high heat until browned and some fat has been rendered. With a slotted spoon, remove and set aside. Add enough oil to equal about 3 tablespoons fat in pot. Sauté onions and cabbage until very soft and slightly brown, about 10 minutes. Stir in sugar and vinegar and cook until vinegar completely evaporates. Add caraway and tomato paste. Cook about 2 minutes. Add stock, bring to a boil, and add potatoes. Reduce heat and simmer 10 minutes. Add beans and reserved hot dogs and cook another 5 minutes. Ladle about ½ cup soup into a small mixing bowl and stir in mustard until smooth. Add mustard mixture to soup and heat through. Taste for salt and pepper and serve.

Serves 8 to 10

LIMA BEAN, LEEK, AND BACON SOUP

This wonderful and unbelievably easy soup has been awarded four stars by one of our most exacting souptasters (who happens to be a relative, we should hasten to add). A lovely, light pale green, the soup tastes as if it has been recklessly thickened with cups of heavy cream when in fact it has none. This is one of those great conversation-piece soups: See which of your guests can guess the base of this rich-tasting purée.

½ pound bacon
2 leeks, white parts only, washed thoroughly
  and chopped
½ teaspoon dried oregano
5 cups Chicken Stock (page 20) or Vegetable
  Stock (page 25)
2 cups cooked lima beans or 1 package
  (10 ounces) frozen lima beans
Salt and pepper
¼ cup chopped chives

In a large heavy saucepan, cook bacon until crisp. Drain on paper towels and crumble. Remove all but 2 tablespoons fat from saucepan and cook leeks until soft, about 6 minutes. Add oregano, stock, and lima beans. Bring to a boil and simmer 15 minutes. In a blender or food processor, purée soup and taste for salt and pepper. Serve sprinkled with bacon and chives.

Serves 8

CRANBERRY BEAN, BUTTERNUT SQUASH, AND CHARD SOUP

Chard is the little magician of this soup, appearing in its two separate guises. Its crunchy stems, crisp as celery, provide substance, while its spinachlike leaves add their bright green freshness. We've heard that Tuscan cooks warn that you cannot make minestrone without *bietole* (chard); so we thought we'd better include it in this minestrone-type mixture. Likewise for the crimson-streaked cranberry beans, which the Tuscans praise for their nutlike, creamy succulence.

---

2 tablespoons vegetable oil
2 leeks, white parts only, thoroughly washed
  and thinly sliced
2 cloves garlic, crushed
½ red onion, chopped
½ teaspoon dried sage
2 cups diced peeled butternut squash
1 bunch chard (about 8 ounces), leaves cut into
  ⅛-inch ribbons and stems cut into 1-inch pieces
6 cups Chicken Stock (page 20) or Vegetable
  Stock (page 25)
2 cups cooked cranberry beans
Salt and pepper
½ cup grated parmesan cheese

In a large heavy pot, heat oil over medium-high heat. Cook leeks, garlic, and onion until soft, about 6 minutes. Stir in sage, squash, and chard stems. Cook another minute. Add stock and simmer 12 minutes. Add beans and chard leaves and cook 10 minutes. Taste for salt and pepper and serve sprinkled with cheese.

Serves 6 to 8

PEARL BARLEY AND RED BEAN SOUP

Like chicken soup, barley broth is supposed to be good for what ails you. Hippocrates considered it something of a magic potion and the ancients seemed to look upon it as a sort of premodern Gatorade. Nor were its gastronomical virtues disparaged; we found one very old recipe which directs the cook to prepare the barley with special vigilance so that none of it goes to waste, and to serve it the moment it is cooked for the ultimate sensual experience. This barley-based soup, with its silky strips of prosciutto and chunky beans, has some of that same old appeal.

---

1 tablespoon vegetable oil
1 onion, chopped
¼ pound prosciutto or country ham, cut into
* thin strips*
2 cloves garlic, minced
6 cups Chicken Stock (page 20)
1 cup pearl barley
½ teaspoon dried marjoram
1 cup corn kernels, fresh or frozen and thawed
1 cup cooked red beans
Salt and pepper

In a large heavy pot, heat oil over medium-high heat. Cook onion, ham, and garlic until onion is soft, about 5 minutes. Stir in stock, barley, and marjoram. Bring to a boil and simmer 30 minutes. Add corn and beans and cook another 10 minutes. Taste for salt and pepper and serve.

Serves 8

Friends have called this creamy, sun-orange purée a magic soup because of its ability to get kids to eat eggplant! Of course, they don't know they're eating it since the eggplant is completely invisible by the time you're finished processing. If you use a good prepared ravioli, you can make this children-friendly soup in minutes.

2 tablespoons olive oil
1 leek, white part only, thoroughly washed
  and chopped
2 small Japanese eggplants, peeled and diced
2 cups chopped tomatoes
1 tablespoon tomato paste
¼ cup chopped fresh parsley
½ teaspoon dried oregano
½ teaspoon dried thyme
6 cups Chicken Stock (page 20) or Vegetable
  Stock (page 25)
Salt and pepper
1 pound cheese ravioli, cooked

In a large heavy nonreactive saucepan, heat oil over medium-high heat. Cook leek and eggplants until soft, about 3 minutes. Stir in tomatoes, tomato paste, parsley, oregano, and thyme. Cook until bubbly, about 4 minutes. Add stock and simmer 30 minutes. Purée in a food processor or in a blender in batches. Taste for salt and pepper. Divide ravioli among 8 soup bowls and ladle soup over them.

Serves 8

NOTES

Entertaining
Soups

Graduation Day, Christmas Eve, the pleasantly crowded block party you finally got around to organizing—these occasions send you scouting for something special. Into this chapter, we've collected the recipes that for one reason or another pack the punch and panache you're looking for. One is memorable because it is baked and served in a pumpkin shell; another is covered with heart-shaped toasts; another is swirled with hard-to-forget horseradish aïoli. Some require a bit of attention and time, but almost all can be prepared completely in advance with only last-minute assembling or reheating. These are not everyday soups, we confess; they are out-of-the-ordinary dishes that herald a special event, a real, honest-to-goodness celebration.

The word *fricassee* usually conjures up memories of Sundays at grandma's or some such homey recollection. But when asked to describe their beloved fricassee, hardly anyone describes the same thing! Some remember a thick, tomatoey stew, others a saffron-yellow chicken and rice dish, still others a creamy casserole. Technically a fricassee means the meat is browned before liquid is added. And although chicken is the most frequently remembered star of this method, anything can be fricasseed from chuck roast to squirrel to lamb's tongue. Our soup-style version is full of reminders of spring, a nice welcome for the family gardener after a morning's planting.

2 tablespoons vegetable oil

1 tablespoon butter

3 pounds skinless and boneless chicken breast,
   cut into 1-inch cubes

Salt and pepper

3 tablespoons flour

½ cup Madeira

6 cups Chicken Stock (page 20)

6 scallions, trimmed and cut into 2-inch lengths

3 medium carrots, quartered lengthwise and
   cut into 2-inch pieces

1 pound asparagus, trimmed and cut into
   2-inch pieces

1 cup heavy cream

¼ cup chopped chives

¼ cup chopped fresh parsley

In a large saucepan, heat oil and butter over medium heat. Season chicken with salt and pepper and cook until it turns white on all sides. Remove and set aside. Add flour to pan and cook, stirring, about 2 minutes. Add Madeira and cook until thick, about 3 minutes. Add stock, bring to a boil, and add scallions and carrots. Simmer 8 minutes. Add asparagus and reserved chicken and simmer another 5 minutes. Stir in cream, heat through, and taste for salt and pepper. Sprinkle with chives and parsley and serve.

Serves 6 to 8

GREAT BIG GUMBO WITH CHICKEN AND SAUSAGE

Like all classics, gumbo is a dish for which there are endless recipes and almost no consensus about the optimal combination of ingredients. In fact, about the only thing most people agree on is that the dish is practically synonymous with Louisiana. However South Carolina takes strong exception to this reputed heritage, contending that okra arrived within its borders with the slave trade prior to the settling of Louisiana. Our version follows the Carolina low country tradition of omitting the filé powder. As for an appropriate occasion, Academy Awards night has just about the right panache.

---

2 chickens (about 3 pounds each)
Flour for dredging
1 pound andouille sausage or other highly
 seasoned smoked sausage, sliced
 ¼ inch thick
Vegetable oil as needed
1 onion, chopped
1 stalk celery, chopped
1 green bell pepper, seeded and chopped
4 scallions, trimmed and chopped

2 cloves garlic, chopped
2 tablespoons flour
1 teaspoon hot pepper sauce, or to taste
1 cup chopped tomatoes
10 cups Chicken Stock (page 20)
1 cup sliced okra
2 cups corn kernels, fresh or frozen and
 thawed
½ cup rice
Salt and pepper

Cut each chicken into 8 pieces and dredge in flour. In a large heavy nonreactive pot, cook sausage until fat is rendered and sausage is brown. Remove with a slotted spoon and set aside. Cook chicken pieces in the same pot until brown all over. This may have to be done in 2 batches. Remove chicken and set aside. Add oil to pan if necessary and stir in onion, celery, green pepper, scallions, and garlic. Cook until soft, about 5 minutes, and stir in flour. Cook until flour turns light brown, about 4 minutes. Add pepper sauce and tomatoes and cook until bubbly. Add stock, okra, and corn. Bring to a boil. Meanwhile remove chicken from bones and cut into small pieces. Add to soup with reserved sausage and rice. Reduce heat and simmer 30 minutes. Taste for salt and pepper and serve.

Serves 12

The popularity of tiny artichokes is no mystery to anyone who has spent hours whittling away at the larger variety. Picked before the fuzzy chokes have formed, these tender vegetables require minimal trimming and fuss. Baby artichokes have been popular since the days of Catherine de Médici, credited with introducing artichokes to France (and therefore, according to the French perspective, to the civilized world). Her favorite recipe was reputed to be artichoke-heart fritters. This easily made soup reminds us of the traditional Greek Easter dish, *mageritsa*. Ours is a lighter, eggless version, which also makes a wonderful starter for Easter Sunday dinner.

1 pound artichoke hearts, fresh or frozen,
  trimmed and quartered
2 leeks, white parts only, thoroughly washed
  and sliced
¼ cup rice
1 teaspoon fresh tarragon leaves or ½ teaspoon
  dried tarragon
2-inch strip lemon zest
5 cups Chicken Stock (page 20) or Vegetable
  Stock (page 25)
Salt and pepper
6 paper-thin slices of lemon

In a large saucepan, combine all ingredients except lemon slices and bring to a boil. Reduce heat and simmer, partly covered, 30 minutes. Remove zest and purée in a food processor or blender. Taste for salt and pepper and serve garnished with lemon slices.

Serves 6

CHUNKY CHICKEN SOUP WITH GREEN BEANS AND ROSEMARY

This rosemary-scented soup whispers hopefully of spring. Full of fresh green beans and drizzled with rosemary oil, it's a good choice for the graduate's luncheon or a bridal shower brunch.

---

2 tablespoons mild flavored olive oil
1 red onion, diced
1 clove garlic, minced
1 stalk celery, diced
1 sprig rosemary or 1 teaspoon dried rosemary
1 pound skinless and boneless chicken breast,
  cut into 1-inch chunks
1 pound red new potatoes, cut into 1-inch cubes
8 cups Chicken Stock (page 20)
1 pound green beans, trimmed and cut into
  1-inch lengths
Salt and pepper
Rosemary oil (page 272)

In a large heavy saucepan, heat olive oil over medium-high heat. Cook onion, garlic, and celery until soft, about 5 minutes. Stir in rosemary and chicken and cook until chicken turns white. Add potatoes and stock, simmer 12 minutes, and add green beans. Simmer another 8 minutes. Taste for salt and pepper. Remove rosemary sprig and drizzle each serving with rosemary oil.

Serves 8

RED, WHITE, AND BLUEBERRY SOUP

For the most patriotic show of colors, we like to serve this berry-spangled soup in white bowls; but red or blue bowls are no less subtle. Needless to say, it makes its most dramatic appearance on the Fourth of July.

3 pints strawberries, quartered
2 pints raspberries
½ to 1 cup sugar, or to taste
1 teaspoon ground cinnamon
1 cup fresh orange juice
¼ cup dry red wine
1 tablespoon grated lemon zest
1 tablespoon grated orange zest
2 cups yogurt
2 tablespoons honey
1 pint blueberries

In a food processor or blender, purée strawberries with raspberries, sugar, cinnamon, orange juice, and wine. Push through a fine-mesh strainer or sieve to get rid of seeds. Pour into a large bowl and whisk in lemon and orange zests and 1 cup of the yogurt until well blended. Combine remaining 1 cup yogurt with honey. Stir blueberries into strawberry mixture. Serve topped with a dollop of honey-yogurt.

Serves 12

CORN AND ZUCCHINI CHOWDER FOR A CROWD

Purists may consider vegetable chowder something like a contradiction in terms, but all chowder fans would agree about one of its essential qualities. Chowder is sociable. In fact, since the earliest days in this country, chowder and the making of it has always been a central event of social gatherings, an entertainment in itself. By the 1820s, chowder parties were common from Boston Harbor to Virginia Beach, often held in conjunction with a political rally. The most populous of these was the record-breaking 10,000 guest chowder feed held in Rhode Island in 1848. This thick summery stew is a good choice for any big happy gathering.

½ pound bacon, diced

2 onions, chopped

1 cup tomatoes, seeded and chopped

1 teaspoon fresh thyme or ½ teaspoon dried
  thyme

½ cup rice

10 cups Vegetable Stock (page 25) or
  Chicken Stock (page 20)

2 pounds zucchini or yellow summer squash,
  cut into ¼-inch cubes

4 cups corn kernels

1 cup milk

Salt and pepper

In a large heavy nonreactive saucepan, cook bacon until crisp. Remove bacon and drain on paper towels. Pour out all but 3 tablespoons fat. Cook onions in the same pan until soft, about 4 minutes. Stir in tomatoes and thyme and cook until bubbly. Stir in rice and cook until well coated with sauce. Add stock, bring to a boil, and add zucchini and corn. Simmer 10 minutes. Remove about 1 cup of the rice-vegetable mixture to a food processor or blender and purée with milk. Return purée to soup and stir well to combine. Stir in reserved bacon. Taste for salt and pepper and serve.

Serves 12

BUTTERNUT SQUASH AND APPLE BISQUE

With its spicy scents of vegetables and fruit, this soup smells like a holiday in progress. Thanksgiving would be an apt occasion for a dish based on an all-American ingredient like butternut squash. Unknown to the rest of the world before Columbus, squash has made its way into a diversity of international dishes from the squash-stuffed ravioli of Italy to the crystallized slices of squash popular in Central America. The final garnish of hot buttery cubes of apple gives a special holiday touch.

3 tablespoons vegetable oil
2 tablespoons chopped shallots
1 stalk celery, chopped
1 Golden Delicious apple, peeled, cored, and
  chopped
½ teaspoon grated nutmeg
½ teaspoon ground cinnamon
3 cups peeled and diced butternut squash
4 cups Chicken Stock (page 20)
¼ cup heavy cream
Salt and pepper

GARNISH
1 tablespoon butter or oil
¼ teaspoon grated nutmeg
¼ teaspoon ground cinnamon
1 large Red Delicious apple, cored and diced

In a heavy medium saucepan, heat oil over medium-high heat. Cook shallots, celery, and apple until soft, about 5 minutes. Stir in nutmeg and cinnamon and cook until fragrant, about 1 minute. Add squash and stock, bring to a boil, and then simmer about 30 minutes or until squash is very tender. In a blender or food processor, purée with cream and taste for salt and pepper.

To make the garnish, in a small skillet, heat butter with nutmeg and cinnamon. Stir in apple and cook 2 minutes. Garnish bowls of soup with apple and serve.

Serves 6

Although the silvery green leaves of sage are rarely seen, their presence is always discernible and nearly universal in holiday stuffings. We've taken advantage of those happy holiday associations, tossing the evocative herb with the croutons that add a crisp counterpoint to this creamy purée.

CROUTONS

4 slices day-old firm-textured white bread
3 tablespoons olive oil
4 fresh sage leaves or ½ teaspoon dried sage

SOUP

1 small onion, chopped
1 acorn squash, peeled, seeded, and cut into
   1-inch cubes
1 sweet potato, peeled and sliced
5 cups Chicken Stock (page 20)
Salt and pepper

To make the croutons, remove crusts from bread and cut into small cubes, about ⅓ inch. Heat oil and sage until hot. Add bread cubes and sauté until golden, tossing frequently. Remove and drain on paper towels.

To make the soup, combine all ingredients in a large saucepan. Bring to a boil, then simmer until vegetables are tender, about 30 minutes. Purée and taste for salt and pepper. Serve topped with croutons.

Serves 6 to 8

GREEN CHILI, BLACK BEAN, AND GOLDEN SQUASH SOUP

This great big chunky mélange is always a favorite with the winter sports set—those who gather around the television set, that is! Most fans enjoy hefting the soup kettle directly into the TV room as an integral part of the pregame festivities. A big loaf of crusty Italian bread (or two) makes a well-appreciated accompaniment.

---

3 tablespoons vegetable oil
6 scallions, trimmed and chopped
2 jalapeño peppers, seeded and cut into thin
  strips
1 Anaheim pepper, seeded and cut into thin
  strips
8 cups Chicken Stock (page 20)
3 cups peeled and cubed (1-inch) winter
  squash such as acorn, pumpkin, Delicata,
  hubbard, or butternut
2 cups cooked black beans
4 ounces angel hair pasta, broken into 2-inch
  lengths
Salt and pepper
½ cup fresh cilantro leaves

In a large heavy pot, heat oil over medium-high heat. Cook scallions and chili peppers until soft, about 5 minutes. Add stock and squash and bring to a boil. Reduce heat and simmer 25 minutes. Add beans and pasta and cook another 8 minutes. Taste for salt and pepper. Sprinkle with cilantro and serve.

Serves 10

Like all squashes, pumpkins are native to America and quickly became staples for the early colonists. "Let no man make a jest at Pumpkins," wrote one of them, "for with this fruit the Lord was pleased to feed his people to their good content, till Corne and Cattell were raised." This black-and-orange dish—tapenade toasts against pumpkin purée—makes a chromatically correct Halloween treat.

SOUP

3 tablespoons olive oil

1 onion, chopped

1 leek, white part only, thoroughly washed
    and chopped

1 stalk celery, chopped

4 cloves garlic, chopped

4 sage leaves or ½ teaspoon dried sage

½ teaspoon crushed red pepper flakes

1 pumpkin (3 to 4 pounds), peeled, seeded,
    and cut into 2-inch cubes

6 cups Chicken Stock (page 20) or water

Salt and pepper

TAPENADE TOASTS

1 cup imported black olives, pitted

2 tablespoons capers, rinsed

4 anchovy fillets

¼ cup shelled walnut pieces

2 sprigs parsley

Grated zest of ½ lemon

Juice of ½ lemon

3 tablespoons olive oil

Salt and pepper

16 to 20 slices baguette, toasted

In a large saucepan, heat oil over medium-high heat. Cook onion, leek, celery, and garlic until soft, about 5 minutes. Stir in sage and red pepper flakes and cook until fragrant. Add pumpkin and stock. Bring to a boil, reduce heat, and simmer until pumpkin is tender, about 45 minutes. Purée in a blender or food processor and taste for salt and pepper.

To make the tapenade toasts, combine all ingredients except baguette slices in a blender or food processor. Process until a rough paste forms. Taste for salt and pepper. Spread tapenade on toasted baguette. Serve soup with tapenade toasts.

Serves 8 to 10

PUMPKIN AND SHRIMP BISQUE BAKED IN A PUMPKIN

For anyone who has looked across a pumpkin field—bumpy acres of plump golden squash—it is hard to imagine a more appropriate symbol of the land of plenty. Cooked and served in one of those giant pumpkin shells, this soup makes a dramatic offering, especially appropriate during the Thanksgiving season.

1 large unblemished pumpkin (about 6 pounds)
Salt and pepper
6 tablespoons butter
1 pound medium shrimp, shelled and deveined
1 large onion, chopped
1 teaspoon fresh tarragon or ½ teaspoon
 dried tarragon

1½ cups dried bread crumbs
4 ounces grated Swiss cheese (1 cup)
6 cups Chicken Stock (page 20)
½ cup heavy cream
½ cup chopped fresh parsley

Preheat the oven to 300 degrees F. With a sharp knife, cut a cover 4 inches in diameter from top of pumpkin. Scrape out seeds and stringy fibers from inside. Sprinkle inside of pumpkin with salt and pepper. In a medium skillet, heat 3 tablespoons butter. Cook shrimp just until they turn pink. Remove with slotted spoon and set aside.

Add remaining butter to skillet and cook onion until soft, about 4 minutes. Stir in tarragon and bread crumbs and cook until butter has been absorbed, about 3 minutes. Remove from heat and stir in cheese. Spoon this mixture into prepared pumpkin. Pour in stock until it reaches 2 inches below rim. Replace pumpkin cover. Place pumpkin on a buttered baking dish and bake until pumpkin begins to soften and soup is bubbling, about 1½ hours. Pumpkin should be tender but still hold its shape.

Remove cover and stir in cream, parsley, and reserved shrimp. Return to oven for another 10 minutes. Taste for salt and pepper. Serve the soup with a scraping of pumpkin.

Serves 8

CABBAGE AND APPLE SOUP WITH RED NEW POTATOES

When you serve this soup, you might want to tell the story of *soupe alexandrine*. It seems that in the nineteenth century, with the expulsion of Napoleon, Russians felt a surge of national pride that extended into the kitchen. Russian cookbooks celebrating traditional Russian dishes began to appear in unprecedented numbers. By midcentury, however, this culinary trend had run its course, and French food returned to fashion. Franco-Russian chefs turned to semantics for the perfect superficial solution; and so it came to pass that an oldtime peasant potage of crab apples and fresh cabbage was renamed *soupe alexandrine*. This is our twentieth-century, back-to-basics interpretation, a warming welcome after an autumn hike or some strenuous cheering at a football game.

---

2 tablespoons vegetable oil
1 large onion, thinly sliced
1 small head savoy cabbage, shredded
2 large tart apples, peeled, cored, and shredded
1 tablespoon brown sugar
1 tablespoon caraway seed
6 cups Chicken Stock (page 20) or
   Vegetable Stock (page 25)

6 small red new potatoes, scrubbed and
   quartered
Salt and pepper
½ cup yogurt or sour cream
¼ cup chopped fresh dill

In a large heavy saucepan, heat oil over medium-high heat. Add onion and cook until soft, about 4 minutes. Add cabbage and apples and cook until soft, about 4 minutes. Stir in brown sugar and caraway seed. Cook until sugar dissolves. Add stock, bring to a boil, add potatoes, and reduce heat. Simmer until potatoes are tender, about 20 minutes. Taste for salt and pepper. Combine yogurt and dill and spoon a dollop over each serving of soup.

Serves 8

Throughout its venerable ten thousand–year history, barley has played an important role in many cultures. In the Middle East barley appears in *belila,* a sweet, souplike syrup served to commemorate a baby's first tooth. Although revered by the Greeks as a fertility symbol, barley was despised by the Romans. In fact, when Roman soldiers were accused of cowardice, their punishment was either death or a diet of barley. Small edible kernels or grains of the grasslike barley plant are covered by a protective inedible husk, which is only partially removed to produce hulled or pot barley. Our recipe uses pearl barley, which is the grain with the outside polished off. This soup is a rich, warming brew which needs only a glass of red wine and a simple salad to make a welcoming supper after a winter walk.

2 tablespoons vegetable oil

2 pounds beef short ribs, excess fat removed

2 onions, chopped

2 carrots, diced

2 stalks celery, sliced

½ cup (1 ounce) dried porcini mushrooms, soaked in 1½ cups hot water 30 minutes

½ pound fresh button mushrooms, sliced

¼ cup tomato paste

3 cups Beef Stock (page 21)

3 cups water

2 cups pearl barley

¼ cup chopped fresh dill weed

Salt and pepper

In a large heavy nonreactive pot, heat oil over medium-high heat. Brown short ribs on all sides. Remove and set aside. Add onions, carrots, and celery and cook until lightly browned and soft, about 10 minutes. Strain dried mushrooms, reserving soaking liquid. Rinse to wash off sand, if any, and add to pot with fresh mushrooms. Cook about 8 minutes. Stir in tomato paste, stock, water, and reserved soaking liquid. Bring to a boil and add barley and reserved short ribs. Reduce heat and simmer, partly covered, 1 hour. Remove ribs from soup and cut meat from bones. Discard bones and return meat to soup. Add dill and cook another 10 minutes. Taste for salt and pepper.

Serves 10

RED PEPPER AND BRUSSELS SPROUT SOUP

Nutritionally speaking, brussels sprouts are almost too good to be true. Full of fiber, folic acid, antioxidants, estrogenic properties, and anticancer indoles, the little cabbage-nuggets are often ignored until holiday time, when they are likely to appear in a dish paired with chestnuts or in a casserole drizzled with maple syrup. In terms of color, Christmas is the perfect occasion for this aromatic green soup appropriately laced with ribbons of red.

2 tablespoons canola oil
¼ cup chopped shallots
1 clove garlic, minced
2 teaspoons grated fresh ginger
1½ pounds brussels sprouts, trimmed of outer
    leaves and chopped
1 small potato, peeled and diced
6 cups Chicken Stock (page 20) or
    Vegetable Stock (page 25)
Salt and pepper

RED PEPPER CREAM
2 red bell peppers, roasted (page 31),
    peeled, and seeded
1 tablespoon honey
Pinch cayenne
1 teaspoon balsamic vinegar
¼ cup heavy cream

In a medium saucepan, heat oil over medium-high heat. Cook shallots, garlic, and ginger over medium heat, until slighly softened, about 4 minutes. Stir in brussels sprouts and cook another 5 minutes. Add potato and stock and bring to a boil. Reduce heat and simmer, partly covered, 20 minutes.

To make the red pepper cream, purée ingredients in a food processor or blender until smooth. When soup is cooked, purée in a food processor or blender until smooth and taste for salt and pepper. Ladle soup into soup bowls and swirl about 2 tablespoons of red pepper purée into each serving.

Serves 6

ENDIVE AND POTATO PURÉE WITH SHREDDED DUCK BREAST

Michael Wild of Oakland's famed Bay Wolf restaurant once served his close friends a five-course, all-duck menu. It began with cheese and "quackers," included a course with mushroom duxelles, and concluded with a duck-egg flan. Needless to say, we all thought the meal was ducky, including the wine which was, appropriately enough, Duxoup (pronounced "duck soup"). For this soup, you don't even need one whole duck. Look for a market that sells only the breast. It may seem extravagant, but this is one of those opulent dishes reserved for close friends and important guests.

---

1 boneless duck breast, cut into ½-inch-wide strips
¼ cup dry vermouth
2 tablespoons chopped shallots
4 heads Belgian endive, cored and shredded
6 cups Chicken Stock (page 20) or
  Duck Stock
2 medium potatoes, peeled and diced
Salt and pepper

Heat a large heavy saucepan about 3 minutes and stir duck strips over medium-high heat until skin is crisp and most of the fat is rendered. Remove duck and set aside. Pour out fat. Return pan to heat and deglaze with vermouth, scraping up brown pieces from bottom. Add shallots and cook about 3 minutes. Stir in endive and cook until wilted. Add stock, bring to a boil, add potatoes, and reduce heat. Simmer until potatoes are tender, about 20 minutes. Purée mixture in a food processor or blender. Taste for salt and pepper. Serve with reserved duck strips as garnish.

Serves 6

CURRIED WINTER SQUASH AND CAULIFLOWER SOUP

The literati who gathered at the Algonquin Hotel in the 1930s were never so involved in haute culture that they forgot about haute cuisine. One of their favorites was a curried concoction called Algonquin Special Soup. So popular was this dish with Gertrude Stein that she requested the recipe from the Algonquin's chef, who provided it, as Alice B. Toklas puts it, "through the kindness of the so amiable maître d'hôtel Georges." Our version of that curried soup is also lovable and warming, especially on a cold December night in front of the fireplace. The bright green leaves of coriander add a spring freshness to this middle-of-winter dish.

---

2 tablespoons vegetable oil
1 onion, chopped
1 stalk celery, chopped
1 pear or apple, peeled, cored, and chopped
1 teaspoon curry powder, or to taste
½ teaspoon ground coriander
6 cups Chicken Stock (page 20) or
   Vegetable Stock (page 25)

3 cups butternut squash, peeled and diced
1 head cauliflower, trimmed and cut
   into florets
1 small potato, peeled and diced
Salt and pepper
½ cup fresh cilantro leaves
½ cup sour cream

In a large heavy saucepan, heat oil over medium-high heat. Cook onion, celery, and pear about 4 minutes. Stir in curry powder and coriander and cook another minute. Add stock and bring to a boil. Add squash, cauliflower, and potato and simmer 20 minutes. Purée in a blender or food processor and taste for salt and pepper. Purée the cilantro leaves with sour cream. Ladle soup into individual bowls. Swirl some cilantro cream into each serving.

Serves 8

SHRIMP BISQUE WITH CAVIAR

This special-occasion dish makes a tantalizing centerpiece for a New Year's Day party. The plump sweet shrimp are always welcome after weeks of often meaty holiday fare. Besides, this bisque is one of the best excuses we know to serve a little extra caviar or even to get rid of any leftover caviar you might have lying around. (Just kidding.)

3 tablespoons butter
1 medium onion, chopped
1 small red bell pepper, seeded and chopped
2 stalks celery, chopped
1 clove garlic, minced
⅛ teaspoon cayenne
⅛ teaspoon dry mustard
1 tablespoon sweet Hungarian paprika
3 tablespoons flour
4 cups Fish Stock (page 24)
1 sprig fresh thyme or ½ teaspoon dried thyme
½ cup heavy cream or half-and-half
½ pound medium shrimp, shelled and deveined
Salt and pepper
¼ cup chopped chives
4 ounces caviar

In a heavy medium saucepan, heat butter over medium heat. Cook onion, pepper, celery, and garlic until soft, about 6 minutes. Stir in cayenne, mustard, paprika, and flour. Cook, stirring, about 2 minutes. Pour in stock slowly, stirring until well blended. Add thyme and bring to a boil. Reduce heat and simmer until thickened about 5 minutes. Add cream and shrimp and cook just until the shrimp turn pink. Taste for salt and pepper. Sprinkle each serving with chives and caviar.

Serves 6

CREAM OF MUSSEL AND SAFFRON SOUP

Any dish that includes saffron presupposes a certain balance and restraint. It makes no sense, gastronomically or economically, to overwhelm the subtle nuances of the world's costliest spice. This expensive reputation is due to the split-second timing required in harvesting the tiny red stigmas of the purple crocus flower, which must be picked within hours of their ripening. In this elegant and rich soup, the ancient spice perfumes both mussels and broth. It's a lovely choice for a small and special New Year's Day gathering.

---

3 tablespoons butter
2 tablespoons chopped shallots
1 clove garlic, minced
¼ cup chopped fresh parsley
1 cup dry white wine
2 pounds mussels, scrubbed
2 cups Fish Stock (page 24) or water
½ teaspoon saffron threads
2 egg yolks
½ cup heavy cream
Salt and pepper

In a heavy medium saucepan, heat butter over medium heat. Cook shallots and garlic until soft, about 4 minutes. Stir in parsley and wine and bring to a boil. Add mussels, cover, and cook, shaking the pan every so often until mussels open. This should take no more than 5 minutes (discard any mussels that do not open). With a slotted spoon, remove mussels and shell them. Add stock to liquid in pot and bring to a boil. Remove from heat and stir in saffron. Combine yolks with cream and whisk into soup until smooth. Return to very low heat and add shelled mussels. Heat gently. Soup should thicken slightly. Taste for salt and pepper and serve.

Serves 4 to 6

Southerners have many imaginative explanations for why they eat this food for the soul every New Year's Day. According to one story, Hoppin' John gets its name because children were required to hop around the table before the holiday meal. In another legend, the dish commemorates a husband who always sprinted to the table the minute supper was ready. Some contend the dish is named for a black cook named John, who had only one leg. Although the dispute continues over the name's origins, there is agreement about Hoppin' John's magical powers: If eaten on New Year's Day, it ensures good luck throughout the year. Whether in a humble home kitchen of the Carolina low country or in an aristocratic Charleston mansion, Southerners make sure to get a plentiful share on the first day of the year.

---

2 tablespoons vegetable oil
4 scallions, trimmed and chopped
About 2 cups diced baked ham
1 bunch kale (about 6 ounces), coarsely chopped
2 cups cooked black-eyed peas
1 cup rice
6 cups Chicken Stock (page 20) or water
Salt and pepper

In a heavy medium saucepan, heat oil over medium-high heat. Cook scallions, ham, and kale about 6 minutes. Add peas, rice, and stock and bring to a boil. Reduce heat and simmer, partly covered, 20 minutes. Taste for salt and pepper and serve.

Serves 6

HALFTIME, HOTTER-THAN-HELL LAMB AND BLACK BEAN CHILI SOUP

Gauntlet-throwing seems inherent to any discussion of chili, from its ingredients to its cooking time. But literally and figuratively, the peppers that go into chili generate the most heat. We use a couple of types in our somewhat unusual lamb-based chili. Anaheims are about six inches long, mild to hot, green or red, and are sometimes called *chiles verdes*. In contrast, jalapeños are small, red when ripe but also sold when mature but green, and range from hot to very hot. But if you want a fiery chili, go for the little habaneros, which are ten times hotter than jalapeños. Crinkly, innocent-looking, and pumpkin colored (though they also come in greens and yellows), habaneros have a deeply aromatic, almost smoky flavor that lingers after the initial fire subsides. They are also known as Scotch Bonnets because they look like highlanders' little hats. This chili makes a very warming meal, especially after a "chilly" Super Bowl game.

---

2 tablespoons vegetable oil
2 onions, chopped
4 cloves garlic, minced
1 red bell pepper, seeded and chopped
1 Anaheim pepper, seeded and chopped
1 to 2 habanero or jalapeño peppers, seeded and chopped
1 teaspoon ground cumin
1 to 2 tablespoons chili powder, or to taste
½ teaspoon dried oregano

½ teaspoon ground mustard seed
2 pounds coarsely ground lamb
1 can (28 ounces) tomatoes, chopped
2 cups Beef Stock (page 21), Lamb Stock (page 27), or water
3 cups cooked black beans
Salt and pepper
½ cup fresh cilantro leaves
2 cups crushed tortilla chips

In a large heavy nonreactive pot, heat the oil over medium-high heat. Add onions, garlic, peppers, cumin, chili powder, oregano, and mustard and cook until vegetables are soft, about 5 minutes. Add lamb and cook, stirring to break up lumps, until raw color disappears. Add tomatoes and stock, stir well to combine, and simmer, partly covered, 45 minutes. Add beans and cook another 10 minutes. Taste for salt and pepper and stir in cilantro. Serve topped with crushed tortilla chips.

Serves 8

Macho-meal—that's what a friend calls this hearty, kettle full of flavor. We have to admit it makes a good centerpiece for everything from poker night to one of those interminable football Sundays.

---

*3 pounds beef round or chuck, trimmed and
 cut into ½-inch cubes*
Salt and pepper
*1 cup finely ground cornmeal mixed with
 3 tablespoons chili powder*
3 tablespoons corn oil
2 large onions, chopped
3 cloves garlic, minced
1 jalapeño pepper, seeded and cut into strips
*1 large red bell pepper, seeded, halved, and
 thinly sliced*

*6 fresh tomatillos, husks removed and
 chopped, or 1 cup canned tomatillos*
*6 plum (Roma) tomatoes, chopped, or 1 cup
 canned tomatoes*
4 cups Beef Stock (page 21)
4 cups water
*3 cups corn kernels, fresh or frozen and
 thawed*
1 cup rice
½ cup fresh cilantro leaves

Sprinkle meat with salt and pepper and dredge in cornmeal mixture. In a large heavy nonreactive pot, heat oil over medium-high heat. Brown beef on all sides. Remove with slotted spoon and set aside. Add more oil to pot if necessary and cook onions, garlic, and peppers until soft, about 5 minutes. Stir in tomatillos and tomatoes. Bring to a boil and cook 3 minutes. Return beef to pot. Add stock and water. Simmer until meat is tender about 1 hour. Add corn and rice and cook another 20 minutes. Taste for salt and pepper and garnish with cilantro.

Serves 10

SWEET ONION–TOMATO CREAM SOUP WITH HERBED HEART TOASTS

Anyone who has traveled in the south of France is familiar with *herbes de Provence*. They come in little unglazed, clay-colored pots in every conceivable size. The words *herbes de Provence* are always written across the pots in a flourish of curly handwriting. The ubiquitous mélange of Provençal herbs has provided many a tourist with the perfect souvenir. Curious about the precise ingredients of the *herbes de Provence* mix, we looked in every imaginable source and could find none. Finally, we looked on the jar. A mixture of thyme, rosemary, tarragon, savory, and basil it said. Can a jar be wrong? In any event, the heart-shaped toasts make this soup a perfect choice for Valentine's Day.

---

1 tablespoon butter or vegetable oil
1 small sweet onion, chopped
1 clove garlic, minced
2 cups drained canned imported Italian
  tomatoes
2 tablespoons honey
1½ cups Chicken Stock (page 20) or
  Vegetable Stock (page 25)
½ cup heavy cream or half-and-half
Salt and pepper

TOASTS
1 teaspoon dried herbes de Provence
1½ tablespoons butter
Salt and pepper
2 slices good quality white bread, cut into
  2-inch hearts with cookie cutter

Preheat the oven to 350 degrees F. In a small skillet, cook *herbes de Provence* in butter about 1 minute. Add salt and pepper to taste. Brush bread hearts with butter mixture on both sides. Place on a baking sheet and bake 8 minutes per side.

In a small heavy nonreactive saucepan, heat butter over medium heat. Cook onion and garlic, until slightly wilted, about 3 minutes. Stir in tomatoes and honey, and cook 5 minutes over medium-high heat. Add stock and simmer 15 minutes. Purée in a food processor or blender with cream and taste for salt and pepper. Ladle into bowls, float heart toasts on top, and serve.

Serves 2

SPLIT PEA, CARROT, AND COUNTRY HAM SOUP

Dried peas have been popular for roughly eight thousand years now, and pea soup is probably the reason. Even as a last-minute decision on an unorganized Sunday afternoon, pea soup is a welcome and warming supper for family and/or friends. We often choose the dried yellow peas to cause some good-natured culinary confusion; people find the taste familiar, but the gold color keeps them guessing.

---

2 tablespoons canola oil
2 cups diced country ham
½ pound baby or miniature carrots,
*   halved lengthwise*
1 onion, chopped
2 cups green or yellow split peas
½ teaspoon dried marjoram
5 cups Chicken Stock (page 20) or water
Salt and pepper
Chopped fresh chervil or chives

In a heavy medium saucepan, heat oil over medium-high heat. Cook ham and carrots until carrots are soft, about 6 minutes. Remove with a slotted spoon and set aside. Cook onion in same pot until soft, about 5 minutes. Stir in peas, marjoram, and stock and bring to a boil. Reduce heat and simmer until peas are tender, about 35 minutes. Purée half the soup in a food processor or blender and return to pot with carrots and ham. Simmer another 10 minutes. Taste for salt and pepper. Sprinkle with chervil and serve.

Serves 8

A GOOD DAY FOR SOUP

Victoria, a friend who was born and raised in Spain, makes paella like someone who was born and raised in Spain. She often gives out her recipe, but when anyone else tries it, the results taste absolutely nothing like hers. Her masterpiece always has that extra and inimitable *"yo no sé que."* Perhaps it is the special Spanish short-grain rice. Or her *paellera*, the dimpled-bottom pan from which paella gets its name. After many delicious experiments, we finally hit upon the perfect solution—soup! This soup conveys the taste, textures, and wonderful little surprises of an original *paella valenciana*.

½ pound chorizo or other spicy sausage, sliced ¼ inch thick

1 skinless and boneless whole chicken breast, cut into ½-inch cubes

½ pound medium shrimp, shelled and deveined

1 onion, chopped

½ red bell pepper, seeded and diced

3 cloves garlic, minced

2 medium tomatoes, seeded and chopped

½ teaspoon saffron threads

½ teaspoon dried thyme

2 tablespoons capers, rinsed

1 cup artichoke hearts, fresh or frozen

1 cup long grain rice

8 cups Chicken Stock (page 20)

2 bay leaves

1 cup peas, fresh or frozen

12 mussels, scrubbed

Salt and pepper

In a large heavy nonreactive pot, cook chorizo until fat is rendered and chorizo is brown. Remove and set aside. You should have about 2 to 3 tablespoons rendered fat left in pot. In same pot, over medium-high heat, sauté chicken and shrimp until chicken turns white and shrimp turn pink, 2 to 3 minutes. Remove and set aside.

Add onion, pepper, and garlic and cook until soft, about 5 minutes. Add tomatoes, saffron, thyme, capers, and artichokes and cook until bubbly. Stir in rice until well coated with sauce. Add stock and bay leaves and bring to a boil. Reduce heat, cover, and simmer 15 minutes. Return sausage, chicken, and shrimp along with peas and mussels to soup and cook until mussels open, about 5 minutes. Taste for salt and pepper, remove bay leaves, and serve.

Serves 12

Meals combining fish and meat have been immortalized, for better or for worse, by American restaurants serving such nostalgia as surf and turf. Actually such mixtures have been popular since Revolutionary times, when beef and oyster sausages were all the rage. But many of the world's cuisines boast perfectly legitimate and venerable *mar y montaña* combos. The Portuguese who settled around Cape Cod's Provincetown, for example, stuff squid with their famous linguiça sausage and also use this sausage with clams in their traditional quahog pie. This soup, which tries to capture that salt-air gusto, can be a hearty main course for a few guests. Smaller portions make a delicious starter.

1 tablespoon olive oil
1 pound linguiça or other garlicky
* sausage, diced*
1 large onion, chopped
1 red bell pepper, seeded and chopped
2 cloves garlic, minced
⅛ teaspoon cayenne
½ teaspoon dried oregano

½ cup white wine
4 cups Chicken Stock (page 20)
4 ounces spaghetti, broken into 2-inch pieces
36 littleneck clams, scrubbed
Salt and pepper
¼ cup chopped fresh parsley

In a large heavy nonreactive saucepan, heat oil over medium-high heat. Add sausage and cook until brown and fat is rendered. Pour off all but 3 tablespoons fat. Stir in onion, pepper, and garlic and cook until soft, about 5 minutes. Add cayenne and oregano and cook another minute. Pour in wine and stock and bring to a boil. Add spaghetti and cook 10 minutes. Add clams and cook until clams open. Discard any unopened clams. Taste for salt and pepper, sprinkle with parsley, and serve.

Serves 6

SICILIAN SPICY FISH SOUP WITH HORSERADISH AÏOLI

In Italy what you call your fish soup depends not on what's in it, but where you are. In southern Italy, it's a *zuppa di pesce*. In the northeastern area called the Marches, the specialty is the Greek-inspired *brodetto*. In Tuscany's Leghorn, south of Pisa, *cacciucco* is a mixture of many fish, including a secret ingredient, *scorfano*, which figuratively means monster. Our version has a few secrets of its own: the invisible but transcendent anchovies and the unorthodox horseradish aïoli. It's a festive choice for a Christmas Eve dinner.

---

3 tablespoons olive oil
1 large onion, chopped
4 cloves garlic, minced
1 large fennel bulb, trimmed, cored, and sliced
½ teaspoon dried thyme
½ teaspoon dried oregano
½ teaspoon crushed red pepper flakes
6 anchovies, drained and mashed
2 cans (28 ounces each) imported Italian
   tomatoes, drained and chopped
2 cups Fish Stock (page 24)
2 pounds assorted white fish, such as
   snapper, sea bass, halibut, or roughy cut
   into 1½-inch chunks

Salt and pepper
½ cup chopped fresh parsley

HORSERADISH AÏOLI
1 cup mayonnaise
2 tablespoons prepared horseradish
1 teaspoon strong mustard
2 tablespoons capers, rinsed and drained

16 slices baguette, toasted (optional)

In a large heavy saucepan, heat oil over medium-high heat. Cook onion, garlic, and fennel until soft, about 8 minutes. Stir in thyme, oregano, red pepper, and anchovies and cook another minute. Add tomatoes and stock and bring to a boil. Reduce heat and simmer, uncovered, 30 minutes. Mixture should thicken and reduce by a fourth.

Meanwhile make aïoli by combining all ingredients until well blended. Add fish to tomato mixture and simmer about 5 minutes. Taste for salt and pepper and stir in parsley. Serve with horseradish aïoli, either stirred directly into each portion of soup or spread on toasts and floated on soup.

Serves 8

"A culinary extravaganza!" that's what Angelo Pellegrini calls minestrone in his book, *The Unprejudiced Palate.* And even though there are millions of minestrones, they all merit that description. Ours is based on an old Neapolitan version, *minestra maritata,* made with pork.

3 tablespoons olive oil

2 pounds pork shoulder, cut into 1-inch cubes

Salt and pepper

2 tablespoons chopped fresh parsley

2 tablespoons chopped fresh basil

½ teaspoon dried thyme

½ teaspoon dried oregano

½ teaspoon crushed red pepper flakes

1 onion, chopped

1 leek, white part only, thoroughly washed and chopped

1 bunch Swiss chard, coarsely chopped

2 cups chopped tomatoes

½ pound dried Great Northern beans, soaked in cold water to cover overnight

½ pound potatoes, peeled and cut into 1-inch cubes

1 large carrot, sliced

1 stalk celery, sliced

1 medium zucchini, sliced

8 cups Beef Stock (page 21) or Chicken Stock (page 20)

Salt and pepper

Grated Parmesan cheese

In a large heavy pot, heat oil over medium-high heat. Sprinkle pork with salt and pepper and brown on all sides. Remove and set aside. In same pot, cook herbs, crushed pepper, onion, leek, and chard about 10 minutes. Stir in tomatoes. Drain beans, stir in, and cook until bubbly. Add potatoes, carrot, celery, zucchini, stock, and reserved pork. Bring to a boil, reduce heat, and then simmer until pork and beans are tender, about 1 hour. Taste for salt and pepper. Serve with a sprinkling of Parmesan cheese.

Serves 12

BROCCOLI, WHITE BEAN, AND SUNDRIED TOMATO SOUP

You've figured out how to program the VCR; you've successfully taped a bunch of those 3 A.M. films; you're set for the night. All you need now are a few fellow movie-freaks and a big tureen of this user-friendly soup. Serve it in big bowls and don't forget the napkins.

---

2 tablespoons olive oil
1 large onion, chopped
2 cloves garlic, chopped
1 carrot, chopped
½ teaspoon dried sage
1½ cups dried Great Northern beans, soaked
   in cold water to cover overnight
5 cups Chicken Stock (page 20)
5 cups water
1 bunch broccoli (about 1½ pounds) peeled
   and cut into small pieces
1 cup chopped sundried tomatoes, oil packed
   or dry
Salt and pepper
½ cup chopped fresh parsley

In a large heavy pot, heat oil over medium-high heat. Cook onion, garlic, and carrot until soft, about 6 minutes. Stir in sage and cook another minute. Drain beans and add with stock and water. Bring to a boil, reduce heat, and then simmer partly covered, until beans are tender, about 1 hour. Add broccoli and tomatoes and cook another 10 minutes. Taste for salt and pepper, sprinkle with parsley, and serve.

Serves 8 to 10

CHILLED BLOODY MARY SOUP

This dish never fails to add a certain dazzle to a dinner party. Its zesty, palate-perking flavors fit in with almost any menu. It is one of the few chilled soups you don't have to reserve for hot weather occasions. In fact, it's always very welcome when the temperature drops, perhaps because the vodka creates a little warmth of its own.

2 tablespoons vegetable oil
1 small sweet onion, chopped
1 stalk celery, chopped
½ teaspoon crushed red pepper flakes
4 cups chopped tomatoes
1 tablespoon honey
2 cups Chicken Stock (page 20)
½ cup vodka
¼ cup fresh lemon juice
2 tablespoons Worcestershire sauce
Salt and pepper
Celery leaves

In a heavy medium nonreactive saucepan, heat oil over medium-high heat. Cook onion and celery until soft, about 5 minutes. Stir in red pepper, tomatoes, and honey. Cook until bubbly. Add stock and bring to a boil. Reduce heat and simmer 15 minutes. Add vodka and simmer another 5 minutes. Pass soup through a food mill. Chill and add lemon juice and Worcestershire sauce. Taste for salt and pepper. Serve with a sprinkling of celery leaves.

Serves 8

NOTES

cold
and
cook-
less

soups

We have filled this chapter with busy-day recipes, soups that can be made almost instantly without even stopping by the stove. Even those recipes that call for minimal cooking are easily and quickly done, making them perfect choices for hot summer nights. For those soups to be served cold, you can hasten the chilling process: Fill a plastic bag with ice cubes and seal well; put the bag in the hot soup and place in the fridge a half hour or so before serving.

Depending on the ingredients, your guests, and your frame of mind, you'll find soups to serve as first courses or light main dishes. The fruit soups make great warm weather desserts. In autumn or winter, a chilled mélange such as spinach, cucumbers, and feta can be an unexpected change of pace.

In recipes that call for buttermilk, yogurt, or sour cream, you can easily substitute one for the other.

They will all provide a rich creaminess, but the degree of tartness will vary. Yogurt is the strongest tasting, followed by buttermilk and sour cream. If you whisk yogurt or sour cream before adding to the soup, they will blend more smoothly. To avoid curdling, let soup mixture cool completely before adding sour cream, yogurt, or buttermilk.

"The cucumber is one of the most valuable vegetables we raise," said the eighteenth-century Shaker *Manifesto* at about the same time that Dr. Samuel Johnson remarked "A cucumber should be...thrown out, as good for nothing." Never noted for his culinary skills, the eminent doctor might have been wrong, judging from the worldwide regard for this food. Cold cucumber soups are popular from the Caribbean, where they often include salt cod or shrimp like our version, to Poland, where the *khlodnik polskii* is usually served with ice cubes, to Russia, where the traditional *okroshka* includes dill, mustard, and scallions, which we have also borrowed here. Although any cucumber will do, you might try the little Kirbys usually reserved for pickling, which add a lovely crispness.

---

6 scallions, trimmed
2 medium cucumbers, peeled and seeded
¼ cup fresh dill sprigs
1 tablespoon Dijon mustard
¼ cup fresh lemon juice
2 cups Vegetable Stock (page 25) or Chicken
  Stock (page 20)
1 tablespoon honey or sugar
1 cup heavy cream
½ pound bay shrimp
Salt and pepper
Dill sprigs

Place scallions, cucumbers, and dill in a food processor or blender. Process until finely chopped. Add remaining ingredients except shrimp, salt, pepper, and dill sprigs and process until smooth. Remove to a bowl and stir in shrimp. Cover and chill until very cold. Taste for salt and pepper, and serve garnished with dill sprigs.

Serves 6

CUCUMBER, RED PEPPER, AND OLIVE SOUP

Roasted peppers, fresh oregano, balsamic vinegar—this cool but lusty soup is full of taste treats. But the real pow comes at the last minute with the big scoop of Greek olives. Thomas Jefferson was right, as always, in his esteem for the olive, which he described as "of all the gifts of heaven to man...next to the most precious, if it be not the most precious." The sensual texture and flavor of olives are the secret to this soup's irresistibility.

1 large hothouse cucumber, peeled, seeded,
    and cut into 2-inch pieces
2 red bell peppers, roasted (page 31), peeled,
    and seeded
2 cloves garlic
2 tablespoons balsamic vinegar
1 teaspoon sugar
1 teaspoon fresh oregano or ½ teaspoon
    dried oregano
¼ cup olive oil
1 cup Vegetable Stock (page 25) or water
¼ cup crème fraîche or sour cream
Salt and pepper
1 cup black Greek olives, pitted and coarsely
    chopped

In a food processor or blender, purée cucumber, peppers, garlic, vinegar, sugar, oregano, oil, stock, and crème fraîche in 2 batches. Pour into a large bowl, cover, and chill. Just before serving, taste for salt and pepper and stir in olives.

Serves 6

SPINACH AND CUCUMBER SOUP WITH FETA CHEESE

Anyone who loves *spanakopita* happily devours this Greek-inspired soup. Its flavor comes principally from feta cheese, which is sprinkled on top. The most commonly available Greek cheese, this white curd cheese is made from either sheep's milk or goat's milk. It gets its tanginess from the brine in which it is pickled to prevent further ripening. If it seems too salty, you can cover it with water overnight before using.

---

2 tablespoons vegetable oil or butter
4 scallions, trimmed and chopped
1 clove garlic, minced
2 medium hothouse cucumbers, peeled, seeded,
  and diced
½ teaspoon dried oregano
1 package (10 ounces) spinach leaves, coarsely
  chopped
½ cup chopped fresh parsley
2 cups Chicken Stock (page 20)
1 tablespoon fresh lemon juice
1 cup buttermilk
Salt and pepper
½ cup crumbled feta cheese

In a medium saucepan, heat oil over medium-high heat. Cook scallions, garlic, and cucumbers until softened, about 5 minutes. Add oregano, spinach, and half the parsley. Cook, stirring, just until spinach wilts. Purée mixture in a blender or food processor with stock and lemon juice. Cover and chill. Stir in buttermilk and taste for salt and pepper. Serve sprinkled with remaining parsley and feta cheese.

Serves 6

YOGURT GAZPACHO

Much as we admire gazpacho in all its cool and alluring guises, we can't resist quoting the French literary figure, Théophile Gautier, who first tasted the soup on a trip to Spain in 1840. He describes the soup as something that "would have made the hair of the late Brillat-Savarin stand on end. . . . A dog of any breeding would refuse to sully its nose with such a compromising mixture." Even the prettiest Andalusian women, he continues incredulously, "do not shrink from swallowing bowlfuls of this hell-broth." In other words, he didn't like it much. We do, especially this lime-laced gazpacho on a summer's day. Be sure to toast the cumin seeds; the way they burst with spicy flavor in contrast with the cold soup is worth the extra few seconds.

---

2 cloves garlic, minced

1 hothouse cucumber, peeled, seeded, and
   chopped

½ small sweet onion, chopped

4 ripe tomatoes, seeded and chopped

1 red or yellow bell pepper, seeded and chopped

1 jalapeño pepper, seeded and chopped

2 tablespoons fresh lime juice

¼ cup olive oil

2 tablespoons cumin seeds, toasted (page 31)
   and crushed

½ teaspoon crushed red pepper flakes

¼ cup fresh cilantro leaves

2 cups tomato juice

1 cup yogurt

Salt and pepper

In a large bowl, combine garlic, cucumber, onion, tomatoes, peppers, lime juice, oil, cumin, red pepper, and cilantro. Stir well and let stand about 1 hour. Purée half the mixture with tomato juice in a blender or food processor. Return to bowl with remaining half and stir well. Stir in yogurt. Cover and chill. Just before serving, taste for salt and pepper.

Serves 6

In her cookbook, Alice B. Toklas tells of her insatiable quest for a gazpacho recipe after sampling versions of the soup in Malaga, Seville, and Cordoba. Indeed, she confesses, the recipes had become "of greater importance than Grecos and Zurburans, than cathedrals and museums." After combing through bookshops and searching endless Spanish cookbooks, she found not one recipe. "Gazpachos," she was told by a bookseller in Seville, "are only eaten in Spain by peasants and Americans." Undaunted, she conducted her own kitchen experiments until she came up with the four varieties in her book. Only too well do we understand that gazpacho frenzy. We make this golden variation when the yellow tomatoes are gold with summer sugar and the peppers are sun-colored, thick, and juicy.

---

*4 large yellow or golden tomatoes, seeded and
  cut up*
*2 yellow or orange bell peppers, quartered and
  seeded*
2 hothouse cucumbers, peeled and seeded
3 cloves garlic
1 small onion, quartered
1 yellow chili pepper, seeded
¼ cup balsamic vinegar
1 teaspoon sugar

¼ cup olive oil
*½ to 1 cup Vegetable Stock (page 25) or
  water*
Dash hot pepper sauce
Salt and pepper
Plain yogurt
Fresh cilantro leaves

Working in batches, in a blender or food processor, purée all ingredients except salt, pepper, yogurt, and cilantro. Cover and chill. Taste for salt and pepper and serve garnished with a dollop of yogurt and cilantro leaves.

Serves 8

GUACAMOLE SOUP

Undoubtedly the hardest thing about this recipe is getting three avocados to ripen on the same day. Once that has been accomplished, this easy soup offers all the delicious advantages of guacamole, plus one. It allows you to use leftover stale tortillas. You heat them in the oven till crisp, place them in a plastic bag, and crush with a rolling pin.

---

3 avocados, halved and peeled
3 ripe tomatoes, halved and seeded
1 jalapeño pepper, seeded
½ teaspoon ground coriander
¼ cup cilantro leaves
Juice of 1 lime
3 cups Chicken Stock (page 20) or Vegetable
  Stock (page 25)
Salt and pepper
1 cup crushed tortilla chips

Place 2½ avocados, 2 tomatoes, jalapeño, coriander, and cilantro in a food processor or blender. Process until fairly smooth. Add lime juice and stock and process until well blended. Dice remaining tomato and avocado and stir into soup. Cover and chill. Taste for salt and pepper and sprinkle each serving with tortilla chips.

Serves 6

TOMATILLO SOUP WITH TOMATO SALSA

Tomatillos are from the same family as tomatoes but come packaged in their own little parchment wrappers. A Mexican favorite since the time of the Aztecs, the tomatillo can be used raw in salads and ceviches or cooked in vegetable dishes and soups. Although it is a real favorite in uncooked salsas, here we have reversed its roles because we like the way a bit of cooking smooths yet enlivens its lemony flavors.

*2 cups chopped husked tomatillos, fresh or
  canned*
½ cup chopped tomatoes, fresh or canned
*2 cups Chicken Stock (page 20) or Vegetable
  Stock (page 25)*
1 tablespoon sugar
½ teaspoon dried oregano
½ cup fresh cilantro leaves
½ cup crème fraîche or heavy cream
Salt and pepper

SALSA
2 medium tomatoes, seeded and chopped
2 scallions, chopped
1 jalapeño pepper, seeded and chopped
¼ cup cilantro leaves, chopped
1 tablespoon fresh lime juice
3 tablespoons olive oil
Salt and pepper

In a medium nonreactive saucepan, combine the tomatillos, tomatoes, stock, sugar, oregano, and cilantro. Cook 10 minutes. Pass through a food mill. Let cool and stir in crème fraîche. Cover and chill.

Meanwhile, combine salsa ingredients in a medium bowl. Just before serving, taste soup for salt and pepper. Serve topped with a spoonful or two of salsa.

Serves 6

EGGPLANT AND RED PEPPER SOUP

At a recent meeting of food writers in San Francisco, a hush fell over the panel when someone asked the eggplant question: to salt or not to salt? Many cooks counsel that, after slicing eggplants, they must be salted to remove bitterness. After some embarrassed hesitation, one of the experts reluctantly admitted that she, in fact, never bothered. The rest of the panel, with smiles of relief, confessed that they also thought salting was a waste of time. You certainly don't have to salt for this recipe. In fact, this very easy soup becomes even easier if you don't peel the eggplant either. The results will be a darker soup with more body.

---

1 medium eggplant, roasted until collapsed
2 medium red peppers, roasted (page 31),
    peeled, and seeded
2 cloves garlic
1 cup tomato juice
2 cups yogurt
Salt and pepper
Chopped fresh parsley

Cut the eggplant into chunks and purée in a blender or food processor with peppers, garlic, and tomato juice. Remove to a bowl and whisk in yogurt. Cover and chill. Taste for salt and pepper and serve sprinkled with chopped parsley.

Serves 6

Mint is summer's favorite trick on the tastebuds. Because it contains menthol, it raises the temperature at which the skin's cold receptors discharge. Simply put, this means that minted foods, like cold soup and drinks, cool the mouth and actually taste colder than they are. In many of the world's cuisines, such as Indian, Thai, and Mexican, this cooling herb is often combined with hot spices to provide relief and counterpoint. This refreshing soup is a welcome first course or lunch dish from May through September; it is really fantastic when you can get farm-fresh peas.

---

4 cups Chicken Stock (page 20)
6 scallions, trimmed and chopped
1 clove garlic, minced
1 pound shelled fresh peas or frozen and thawed peas
1 sprig fresh thyme or ¼ teaspoon dried thyme
1 teaspoon sugar
12 mint leaves
2 tablespoons fresh lemon juice
1 cup yogurt or sour cream
Salt and pepper

In a medium saucepan, bring stock to a boil. Add scallions and garlic and cook 5 minutes. Add peas, thyme, sugar, and mint and cook until peas are tender, about 8 minutes. Purée mixture in a blender or food processor. Stir in lemon juice and sour cream, cover, and chill. Just before serving, taste for salt and pepper.

Serves 8

CHILLED HERB SOUP

When just about everybody likes a thing, you have to be a little suspicious. So we were concerned when no one—not even a few recipe-testing teens—had any complaints about this soup. Of course, the soup fits right in with today's emphasis on simple cooking and natural ingredients with their intrinsic flavors intact. And it gives you a chance to gather those bunches of herbs from your garden or produce market and use lots of them, not just a pinch or a last-minute superficial sprinkling. In combination, this mixture of herbs yields a lively, fresh-tasting mélange full of subtle, well-tempered flavors. In some ways, the whole thing sounds a little too trendy. On the other hand, it tastes terrific. Maybe that's why everybody likes it.

---

2 tablespoons butter or vegetable oil
2 shallots, minced
½ cup chopped chives
½ cup chopped fresh parsley
½ cup chopped fresh chervil
2 tablespoons chopped fresh tarragon
2 tablespoons chopped fresh dill
1 tablespoon grated lemon zest
2 cups Chicken Stock (page 20)
1 cup milk
½ pound potatoes, peeled and cooked
Salt and pepper
Mixed chopped herbs

In a medium saucepan, heat butter over medium heat. Add shallots, chives, parsley, chervil, tarragon, dill, and lemon zest. Cook about 2 minutes. Add stock, bring to a boil, and cook 2 minutes. In a blender or food processor, purée herb mixture with milk and potatoes. Cover and chill. Just before serving, taste for salt and pepper and garnish with chopped herbs.

Serves 4

CREAM OF MIXED LETTUCES WITH CHIVES AND CHERVIL

In the Transylvanian mountains around Sibiu, Romania, there lives a certain group of people whose appearance can only be called startling. Unlike their neighbors, the robust looking, blue-eyed blonds are Saxons who emigrated eight centuries ago from Saxony. An important part of their heritage is *Salatsuppe,* or salad soup, based on just about any mixture of lettuces around. For our interpretation, we've lightened the original, slipping in some herbs in place of eggs and butter. But only a Sibiu Saxon will know for sure.

---

4 cups Chicken Stock (page 20) or Vegetable
  Stock (page 25)
8 cups mixed coarsely shredded lettuces
½ cup half-and-half
Salt and pepper
¼ cup finely chopped fresh chervil
¼ cup finely chopped chives

In a large pot, bring stock to a boil. Add lettuces, poking leaves down. Cook until wilted, about 8 minutes. With a slotted spoon remove lettuces to a food processor or blender. Purée with some stock. In a large bowl, combine remaining stock with purée. Cover and chill until very cold. Stir in half-and-half and taste for salt and pepper. Sprinkle with chervil and chives and serve.

Serves 6

The only problem with sorrel soup is getting hold of enough sorrel. Those inclined to garden will find sorrel thrives as heartily as a weed, and for good botanical reasons. Wild sorrel was one of the edible wild plants the early colonists learned about from Native Americans, who used it to flavor their soups. In fact, soup is almost an inevitable destiny for sorrel, which seems to liquefy in the presence of moisture and heat. Perhaps that's why almost every culture has its version of sorrel soup, from the French *potage à l'oseille* (often served hot) and *potage Germiny* (usually served cold) to the German *Sauerampfersuppe;* and from the old Shaker Sister Amelia's herb soup to the ageless Jewish Shav. This is our cucumbered version.

---

1 pound sorrel, coarsely chopped
6 scallions, trimmed and chopped
8 cups water
1 egg, beaten
1½ cups sour cream
Salt and pepper
1 pound small red new potatoes, scrubbed,
  cooked, and diced
1 medium cucumber, peeled, seeded, and diced

In a large saucepan, simmer sorrel and scallions in the water about 20 minutes. Whisk about 1 cup soup into egg until well blended. Whisk egg mixture back into soup. Remove to a bowl, cover, and chill. Stir in sour cream until well blended and taste for salt and pepper. Add potatoes and cucumber and serve.

Serves 6

COLD AND COOKLESS SOUPS

Among the most intriguingly named seafood dishes in this country is Charleston she-crab soup. This is not discrimination; it's just that only the she-crabs carry the delicious roe inside. To even things out, perhaps, on the West Coast, where the fine-flavored Dungeness crab is a matter of Pacific pride, only the male is used. Almost any species—from the red crabs of Gloucester, Massachusetts, to the long-legged Alaskan Kings, whose sweet meat is often frozen on board fresh from the tangle nets—will work in this elegant and easy soup.

---

2 tablespoons oil
2 tablespoons chopped shallots
1 tablespoon curry powder, or to taste
Pinch cayenne
¼ teaspoon ground coriander
3 tablespoons flour
4 cups tomatoes, chopped
½ cup Chicken Stock (page 20)
½ cup half-and-half
Salt and pepper
1½ cups cooked crab meat
½ cup chopped chives

In a medium-size nonreactive saucepan, heat oil over medium-high heat. Cook shallots until translucent, about 3 minutes. Stir in curry, cayenne, coriander, and flour. Cook over low heat about 3 minutes. Stir in tomatoes and stock and bring to a boil. Reduce heat and simmer 15 minutes. Pass soup through a food mill. Cover, chill, and stir in half-and-half. Taste for salt and pepper. Serve garnished with crab and chives.

Serves 8

CHILLED PEAR AND PARSLEY SOUP

The natural perfume of pears makes this soup a haunting and sophisticated first course, particularly in cool weather when pears are common but cold soups are not. Any juicy, buttery-fleshed pear works beautifully here; avoid storage pears, which can impart an off flavor. In late summer, Bartletts are perfect.

---

6 ripe pears, peeled, cored, and cut into thin wedges
½ teaspoon ground cinnamon
½ teaspoon freshly grated nutmeg
2 tablespoons sugar
2 tablespoons fresh lemon juice
3 tablespoons rice
½ cup half-and-half, milk, or sour cream
½ cup chopped fresh parsley

In a medium saucepan, combine pears, cinnamon, nutmeg, sugar, lemon juice, and rice. Cover with water and simmer until pears are tender, about 15 minutes. Let cool. In a blender, purée pear mixture with half-and-half and ¼ cup parsley. Cover and chill. Just before serving, taste for sugar and lemon juice. Sprinkle with remaining parsley.

Serves 6

MELON AND MELON SEED PASTA SOUP

This soup may sound very poetic—and it is! But there's more to poetry than meets the ear, as you'll see when you serve this unusual fruit soup. Its complex taste, slightly peppery and spiked with fresh basil, is enhanced by the melon's sweetness. For extra intrigue, we sometimes use yellow watermelon, which gives the soup a familiar watermelon taste without the expected rosy color.

---

1 large hothouse cucumber, peeled, seeded,
*   and cut into 2-inch pieces*
2 cups cantaloupe chunks
4 cups watermelon chunks, seeded
1 cup yogurt
⅛ teaspoon cayenne
Pinch salt
2 tablespoons chopped fresh basil
1 cup cooked melon seed pasta

In a blender or food processor, purée cucumber, cantaloupe, watermelon, yogurt, and cayenne in 2 batches. Pour into serving bowl, cover, and chill. Just before serving, taste for salt and stir in basil and pasta.

Serves 6

MIXED MELON AND PROSCIUTTO SOUP

When Bartolomeo de Sacchi, the fifteenth-century Vatican librarian, got tired of cataloguing books, he wrote one of his own. In fact, his *Platina De honesta voluptate* was the first signed cookbook published since the ancient Roman era. One of his most welcome innovations was an emphasis on fresh fruit to begin a meal, a concept immortalized in such popular hors d'oeuvres as figs or melon with prosciutto. This soup is a spoonable variation on Platina's theme.

---

1 small ripe cantaloupe, seeded, peeled,
* and cut into chunks*
1 small ripe honeydew, seeded, peeled,
* and cut into chunks*
¼ cup fresh parsley leaves
¼ cup white wine
2 tablespoons Cointreau
3 tablespoons fresh lemon juice
¼ cup heavy cream
Salt and pepper
2 ounces prosciutto, cut into strips

Purée melons and parsley until smooth in a food processor or blender. Transfer to a bowl and stir in wine, Cointreau, lemon juice, and cream. Cover and chill. Taste for salt and pepper and serve topped with prosciutto strips.

Serves 4

Tell your guests that this lush blend of avocado and melon is a fruit soup and they will spend the whole soup course tasting very carefully. Chances are no one will be able to track down the causes of its tantalizing nutty sweetness. Be prepared to have someone call "Foul!" when you reveal the presence of avocado because most people don't think of avocado as a fruit. Undoubtedly they'll forgive you for that slightly misleading clue and probably even ask for the recipe.

---

2 large avocados, peeled, pitted, and cut into
  small chunks
½ cup fresh lemon juice
½ cup fresh orange juice
1 cup arugula leaves, coarsely shredded
1 cup diced ripe cantaloupe
1 cup Chicken Stock (page 20)
1 cup half-and-half or heavy cream
Salt and pepper

Purée avocados in a food processor or blender with lemon juice, orange juice, half the arugula, half the cantaloupe, and stock. Pour into serving bowl and stir in half-and-half. Cover and chill. Just before serving, taste for salt and pepper. Garnish with remaining arugula and cantaloupe.

Serves 6

MANGO AND AVOCADO SOUP

Avocado and fresh ginger is a favorite Caribbean combination, which flavors island soups based on everything from strawberries to passion fruit to mixtures of fresh citrus. Thus inspired, we offer this cooling, pale green purée which, in true tropical spirit, requires no cooking at all.

---

*2 medium avocados, peeled, pitted, and cut
  into chunks*
1 large mango, peeled and cut into chunks
1 tablespoon grated fresh ginger
1 tablespoon honey, or to taste
1 lime
1 cup fresh orange juice
½ cup pineapple juice
1 cup yogurt or buttermilk

Combine avocados, mango, ginger, and honey in a food processor or blender. Process until smooth. Grate exterior of lime to get about 1 tablespoon zest and set aside. Squeeze juice from lime, and add it and orange and pineapple juices to mango mixture. Process again until smooth. Remove to a bowl and stir in the yogurt. Cover and chill until very cold. Garnish with lime zest and serve.

Serves 6

ICED TOMATO AND RHUBARB SOUP

Your guests will probably never guess the origin of the complex acid tastes of this wonderfully flavored dish. It's based on one of the innumerable versions of a Persian *khoresh* (a stewlike topping for rice), in this case a sweet and acid rhubarb sauce spiked with cinnamon. This soup gives rhubarb lovers something to make besides pies and crumbles.

---

1 pound rhubarb, sliced ½ inch thick
2 tablespoons brown sugar
½ cup granulated sugar
½ teaspoon ground cinnamon
1 pound ripe tomatoes, seeded and chopped
1 cup Chicken Stock (page 20)
1 cup tomato juice
1 teaspoon fresh thyme or ½ teaspoon dried
  thyme
Salt and pepper
1 tablespoon chopped chives
2 tablespoons chopped fresh parsley

In a medium-size nonreactive saucepan, combine rhubarb with sugars and cinnamon. Cover and cook until rhubarb begins to soften, about 8 minutes. Add tomatoes and cook another 5 minutes. Stir in stock, tomato juice, and thyme. Bring to a boil, reduce heat, and simmer, uncovered, until mixture turns liquid and pieces of rhubarb disintegrate. Purée in a blender or food processor. Cover and chill. Taste for salt and pepper. Sprinkle with chives and parsley and serve.

Serves 6

PLUM SOUP WITH CINNAMON AND ALMONDS

This soup is the result of one of those summer drives in the country where farm stands seem to sprout up every other mile. Who could resist the chance to buy half a dozen varieties of plums, just a handful of each? But after a few days of plum cobblers, puddings, and tarts, serious plum cooking was in order. Of course there are jam and chutney, but this soup was one of the simplest and everyone's favorite for outright plumminess. Italian prune-plums or any freestone variety are the easiest to pit. They contrast deliciously with the crushed toasted almonds that both thicken and flavor the soup.

---

2 pounds plums, quartered and pitted
3 tablespoons brown sugar
1 teaspoon ground cinnamon
Grated zest of ½ orange
Grated zest of ½ lemon
2 cups fresh orange juice
2 tablespoons fresh lemon juice
1 cup almonds, toasted (page 31)
  and coarsely chopped
½ to 1 cup water

In a medium saucepan, combine plums, brown sugar, cinnamon, orange and lemon zests, with just enough water to cover. Simmer, partly covered, until plums break down, about 12 minutes. Allow to cool slightly. In a blender or food processor, purée plum mixture with orange juice, lemon juice, half the almonds, and ½ to 1 cup water. Cover and chill. Serve sprinkled with remaining almonds.

Serves 4 to 6

Don't say we didn't warn you, but "plum good" is the almost irresistible plum pun that this soup almost inevitably inspires. It's worth the risk, however, to enjoy the peppery sweetness of this watercress-fruit combination, based on an old Kansas Mennonite *Pflaumensuppe* (plum soup) recipe, which got its tartness from rhubarb.

---

3 pounds ripe plums, quartered and pitted
2 bunches (6 ounces each) watercress leaves
4 cups Chicken Stock (page 20)
3 tablespoons fresh lemon juice
¼ cup heavy cream or half-and-half
Salt and pepper

In a medium saucepan, simmer plums, three-fourths of the watercress, and stock about 10 minutes. Purée in a food processor or blender until smooth. Cover and chill. Stir in lemon juice and cream and taste for salt and pepper. Garnish each serving with remaining watercress leaves.

Serves 6

GINGERED CARROT AND APRICOT SOUP

When the weather begins to warm and our culinary thoughts start turning to visions of fruit soup, the first one we think of is this apricot delight. Maybe that's because the apricot is one of the first of summer's cornucopia to ripen. In fact the early roots of the word apricot are from the Latin word *praecoquere* (to ripen early), which is also the root for precocious. Carrots and orange juice deepen the colors of this ginger-flecked spring perennial.

---

4 large carrots, sliced and cooked until tender
1 cup diced ripe apricots
2 tablespoons minced fresh ginger
2 tablespoons brown sugar
Pinch cayenne
¼ cup fresh lemon juice
1 cup fresh orange juice
2 cups Chicken Stock (page 20) or water
Chopped fresh cilantro

In a blender or food processor, purée carrots, apricots, ginger, sugar, cayenne, lemon and orange juice, and stock. Cover and chill. Serve sprinkled with cilantro.

Serves 4 to 6

The fifteenth-century Venetian painter Giovanni Bellini would undoubtedly be dismayed to learn which Venice masterpiece his name calls to mind. These days, the most well-known Bellini may well be the peach-champagne drink ordered repeatedly at Harry's Bar by thirsty tourists, tired from counting pigeons on the Piazza San Marco and chopping through the Grand Canal in a hot-rodder *vaporetto*. The Bellini and its Venetian connotations make this soup a good memory even before you taste it, but don't let that stop you.

---

8 ripe peaches, peeled, pitted, and quartered
½ cup fresh orange juice
2 tablespoons fresh lemon juice
2 tablespoons brown sugar, or to taste
2 cups Champagne or sparkling white wine
1 cup light sour cream
6 mint sprigs

In a blender or food processor, purée peaches, orange and lemon juice, and sugar until smooth. Stir in Champagne and sour cream until well blended. Cover and chill until very cold. Serve garnished with mint sprigs.

Serves 6

NOTES

soups

Sometimes it's nice not to have to make a choice. With this varied selection of slender soups, for example, you don't have to choose between something that's good for you and something that's good. No wonder the "soup diet" has become so popular. In fact, a study at the University of Pennsylvania showed that people who began their meal with soup ate less and consumed fewer calories. Almost any soup can be lightened with a little judicious handling. Sauté vegetables in nonstick pans or regular pans sprayed with a vegetable spray. Or put vegetables in a microwave with a little water. Thicken soups with a cooked potato puréed into the mix, or stir up some instant mashed potato. You can almost always substitute nonfat yogurt for sour cream, nonfat milk for regular. You can sometimes eliminate cream by using milk thickened with a little cornstarch.

These slender soups get their appeal from alluring spices like saffron and curry, the inviting texture of shaped pastas, and the richness of thickened vegetable purées.

CREAM OF CAULIFLOWER, LEEK, AND SPINACH

The cool green color of this light soup makes it especially inviting, crisscrossed as it is with shreds of fresh spinach. We sometimes use green cauliflower, which produces a much darker purée. Either way, this fragrantly spiced soup is a treat.

---

1 medium head cauliflower, coarsely chopped
3 leeks, white parts only, thoroughly washed
  and sliced
2 cloves garlic, minced
5 cups Chicken Stock (page 20) or Vegetable
  Stock (page 25)
1 teaspoon cumin seed, toasted (page 31)
½ teaspoon grated nutmeg
⅛ teaspoon cayenne
6 ounces (6 cups) fresh spinach, coarsely chopped
Salt and pepper

In a large saucepan, combine cauliflower, leeks, garlic, and stock. Bring to a boil, reduce heat, and simmer, uncovered, until vegetables are tender, about 15 minutes. Add cumin, nutmeg, cayenne, and half the spinach. Cook another 5 minutes. Purée in a blender or food processor. Reheat with remaining spinach. Taste for salt and pepper and serve.

Serves 6

SAFFRONED CAULIFLOWER AND ONION SOUP

Here cauliflower makes a delightful soup for the weight conscious, especially when puréed into creaminess with a single potato. Saffron elevates the dish into elegance and tints it a beautiful rich ocher.

---

2 tablespoons vegetable oil
1 large sweet onion, chopped
¼ cup chopped shallots
½ teaspoon saffron threads
¼ teaspoon ground turmeric
1 medium head cauliflower, chopped
4 cups Chicken Stock (page 20)
1 large all-purpose potato, peeled and diced
Salt and pepper
¼ cup chopped chives

In a heavy medium saucepan, heat oil over medium-high heat. Cook onion and shallots until very soft, about 7 minutes. Stir in saffron and turmeric and cook another minute. Add cauliflower and stir until coated with onion-saffron mixture, about 2 minutes. Add stock, bring to a boil, and add potato. Simmer until vegetables are tender, about 20 minutes. In a blender or food processor, purée mixture. Taste for salt and pepper. Serve garnished with chives.

Serves 6

BROCCOLI BUTTERMILK SOUP WITH TOASTED ALMONDS

Like an old friend, broccoli always seems to be there for you, full of goodness and possibility. Whatever the season or the circumstances, you can find it, green and bulging, near the center of the produce department. Neither assertive nor bland, broccoli offers more, nutritionally, than just about any other commonly consumed vegetable. In this lush purée, it takes on the pepperiness of watercress, the tang of buttermilk, and the toasty warmth of the almonds used to thicken it.

---

2 tablespoons canola oil
1 onion, chopped
1 clove garlic, minced
2 cups Chicken Stock (page 20) or Vegetable
  Stock (page 25)
½ pound broccoli, stems sliced and florets
  left whole
1 cup (4 ounces) almonds, toasted (page 31)
  and chopped
½ cup watercress leaves
½ cup buttermilk
Salt and pepper

In a heavy medium saucepan, heat oil over medium-high heat. Cook onion and garlic until wilted, about 5 minutes. Add stock, bring to a boil, and stir in broccoli stems and all but 4 of the florets. Add almonds. Cook until broccoli is tender, about 8 minutes. In a blender or food processor, purée broccoli with watercress. Return to pot and stir in buttermilk. Reheat gently. Taste for salt and pepper. Serve garnished with reserved florets.

Serves 4

If (or should we say when?) soup for breakfast becomes the latest trend, this bright-tasting combination could help rouse the drowsiest taste buds. Meanwhile, don't hesitate to serve up a big chilled or steaming bowl any old time, especially when you're looking for one of those magical potions that is thick and rich and totally guilt-free.

4 cups Chicken Stock (page 20) or
    Vegetable Stock (page 25)
1½ pounds carrots, sliced
1 parsnip, peeled and sliced → omit
2 shallots, chopped   X 3
½ onion, chopped
½ teaspoon dried thyme or 1 teaspoon
    fresh thyme
2 tablespoons honey
½ cup fresh orange juice
1 tablespoon fresh lemon juice
Salt and pepper
6 orange or lemon slices

In a medium saucepan, bring stock to a boil. Add carrots, parsnip, shallots, onion, thyme, and honey. Reduce heat and simmer, covered, 30 minutes. Remove vegetables with a slotted spoon to a food processor or, in 2 batches, to a blender. Purée with orange and lemon juice. Add remaining soup and process again until smooth. Taste for salt and pepper. Serve garnished with orange slices.

May be served hot or chilled.

Serves 6

What makes this soup special is the counterplay of sweet carrots and sour sorrel. Make it on a day when the carrot man shows up at the farmers' market with his sweetest harvest, and you will marvel at the extra dimension that just-picked ingredients can provide. This soup is a rich-tasting dish for lunch or dinner.

---

2 tablespoons vegetable oil
1 medium sweet onion, chopped
1 teaspoon fresh marjoram or ½ teaspoon
  dried marjoram
¾ pound sorrel, coarsely chopped
4 cups Chicken Stock (page 20) or Vegetable
  Stock (page 25)
1 pound carrots, sliced
½ pound all-purpose potatoes, peeled
  and diced
Salt and pepper

In a large heavy saucepan, heat oil over medium-high heat. Cook onion, marjoram, and sorrel until vegetables are wilted, about 5 minutes. Add stock, bring to a boil, and add carrots and potatoes. Reduce heat and simmer 20 minutes. Remove about a third of mixture to a blender or food processor and purée. Return to remaining soup in pot and stir well to combine. If soup is too thick, add water or stock to thin. Taste for salt and pepper and serve.

Serves 6

Almost every kid enjoys nibbling on a handful of Kentucky Wonders or snappy Blue Lakes as if they were french fries. This basically potato soup is really that very childhood treat in disguise, since the beans are fresh, bite size, and barely cooked.

---

2 tablespoons olive oil
1 large onion, chopped
1 clove garlic, minced
¼ pound red new potatoes, scrubbed and diced
5 cups Chicken Stock (page 20) or water
½ cup basil leaves, cut into strips
1 pound green beans, cut into 1-inch pieces
Salt and pepper

In a large heavy saucepan, heat oil over medium-high heat. Cook onion and garlic until soft, about 5 minutes. Add potatoes and cook another 5 minutes. Stir in stock, bring to a boil, reduce heat, and simmer, covered, 25 minutes. In a blender or food processor, purée about a ladleful of soup with half the basil and return to soup. Stir well to combine. Add green beans and cook about 5 minutes. Taste for salt and pepper. Serve garnished with remaining basil.

Serves 6

This time the rice has it: the ability to enrich and thicken without added cream or fat. In fact, because you purée only half of the mixture, the final soup looks as chunky as a hearty stew—well, almost.

---

2 tablespoons oil
4 scallions, trimmed and sliced
1 ounce prosciutto, diced
4 tablespoons Arborio rice
1 teaspoon fresh oregano or ½ teaspoon
   dried oregano
4 to 5 cups Chicken Stock (page 20) or
   Vegetable Stock (page 25)
2 green zucchini, diced
2 yellow summer squash, diced
Salt and pepper

In a medium saucepan, heat oil over medium-high heat. Sauté scallions and prosciutto until scallions are soft, about 4 minutes. Stir in rice and oregano and cook until rice becomes transluscent, about 2 minutes. Add stock, bring to a boil, and add zucchini and squash. Simmer, partly covered, 15 minutes. Purée half the mixture in a food processor or blender and return to remaining mixture in saucepan. Stir until well combined. Taste for salt and pepper and serve.

Serves 6

MINTED SUMMER SQUASH SOUP WITH ANGEL HAIR PASTA

Mint is a favorite herb in Sicily and parts of southern Italy, where several kinds are popular in vegetables, lamb dishes, and even cheese frittatas. Its tangy flavor becomes much more subtle when it is cooked, as in this luscious but light pasta soup.

---

2 tablespoons butter or vegetable oil
4 cloves garlic, thinly sliced
½ teaspoon crushed red pepper flakes
4 zucchini or summer squash, quartered
   lengthwise and sliced ½ inch thick
5 cups Vegetable Stock (page 25) or Chicken
   Stock (page 20)
4 ounces angel hair pasta, broken into
   1-inch pieces
2 tablespoons chopped fresh mint
2 tablespoons chopped fresh parsley
Salt and pepper

In a large heavy pot, heat butter over medium heat. Cook garlic and red pepper about 3 minutes. Add zucchini and cook, stirring, about 2 minutes. Add stock, bring to a boil, and add pasta. Cook 5 minutes and stir in mint and parsley. Cook another minute. Taste for salt and pepper and serve.

Serves 6

FENNEL AND LEEK VICHYSSOISE

Like a plain boiled potato, vichyssoise tempts the color-conscious cook to add a frizzle of parsley or a tinge of paprika or saffron. And yet vichyssoise makes a supreme case for leaving well enough alone. We almost succeeded, until one day when the fennel was too fresh and fragrant to ignore. It seemed only right for this slendersoup, especially since fennel is sometimes called the "slimming herb."

---

3 tablespoons light-flavored olive oil

*4 leeks, white parts only, thoroughly washed
  and chopped*

2 cloves garlic, minced

1 tablespoon crushed fennel seed

*2 large fennel bulbs, trimmed and chopped,
  feathery stalks chopped and reserved*

*4 cups Chicken Stock (page 20) or Vegetable
  Stock (page 25)*

2 medium potatoes, peeled and diced

Salt and pepper

¼ cup low-fat sour cream

In a medium saucepan, heat oil over medium-high heat. Cook leeks, garlic, fennel seed, and fennel, covered, over low heat, until vegetables are very soft, about 15 minutes. Add stock and potatoes, bring to a boil, reduce heat, and simmer, partly covered, another 15 minutes. Purée in a food processor or blender. Taste soup for salt and pepper. Swirl in sour cream and garnish with the reserved chopped feathery stalks.

Serves 6

FOUR FISH AND FENNEL SOUP

Although this fish and seafood mélange seems extravagant, the most virtuous dieter may dine on it with impunity. Flavored with fennel, which some say magically breaks down oils and fats, it is really a light and lusty whole meal in a bowl.

---

2 tablespoons olive oil
2 tablespoons fennel seed, crushed
2 cloves garlic, minced
1 small red onion, chopped
½ teaspoon crushed red pepper flakes
3 large bulbs fennel, trimmed, cored, and
   thinly sliced
2 large tomatoes, seeded, and coarsely chopped
5 cups Fish Stock (page 24) or
   Chicken Stock (page 20)
1 pound red new potatoes, scrubbed and diced

½ pound salmon fillet, skinned and cut into
   1-inch chunks
½ pound snapper or halibut fillet, cut into
   1-inch chunks
½ pound medium shrimp, shelled and
   deveined
½ pound bay scallops
Salt and pepper

In a large heavy nonreactive pot, heat oil over medium-high heat. Add fennel seed, garlic, onion, red pepper, and fennel and cook about 8 minutes. Stir in tomatoes and cook until bubbly. Add stock, bring to a boil, and add potatoes. Reduce heat and cook until potatoes are tender, about 15 minutes. Add salmon and snapper, simmer 3 minutes, and then add the shrimp and scallops. Simmer another 3 minutes. Taste for salt and pepper and serve.

Serves 6

ASPARAGUS, PEA, AND SHRIMP SOUP WITH LEMONGRASS

Asparagus lovers, like us, are always looking for new ways to capture the season before it slips away. This Thai-inspired dish is a delicious solution, which also takes advantage of summer's first basil.

---

6 cups Chicken Stock (page 20)
3 stalks lemongrass, tender parts only, cut
*   into 2-inch lengths*
2 jalapeño peppers, seeded and thinly sliced
1½ cups peas, fresh or frozen
1 pound thin asparagus, trimmed and cut
*   into 2-inch lengths*
1 pound medium shrimp, shelled and deveined
4 scallions, trimmed and thinly sliced
10 small fresh basil leaves
¼ cup fresh lime juice
¼ cup coarsely chopped fresh cilantro leaves
Salt and pepper

In a large saucepan, bring stock to a boil. Add lemongrass and jalapeños and boil 3 minutes. Add peas and asparagus and cook 3 minutes. Add shrimp and cook 2 minutes. Stir in scallions, basil, lime juice, and cilantro. Taste for salt and pepper and serve.

Serves 6

CURRIED CHICKEN CHOWDER

Proponents of nouvelle cuisine, spa menus, and so-called light cooking have reached at least one common conclusion: Even the most scrupulous dieter can't live without flavor. Using assertive spices, exotic herbs, "new" vegetables like broccoli raab and bok choy, and all degrees of hot peppers, today's cook can produce appealing dishes with complex and intriguing flavors and minimal fat. This soup, with its curry and apples, tomatoes and coriander, is a tasty example, fit for anyone from marathon runner to pleasure-driven gourmand.

---

2 tablespoons canola oil
1 medium onion, chopped
2 cloves garlic, minced
1 stalk celery, chopped
1 carrot, chopped
1 medium apple, cored and chopped
1 tablespoon curry powder, or to taste
1 teaspoon ground coriander
½ teaspoon ground cumin
½ teaspoon turmeric (optional)

2 tablespoons flour
½ cup chopped tomatoes
2 medium potatoes, peeled and diced
6 cups Chicken Stock (page 20) or
  Vegetable Stock (page 25)
1½ pounds skinless and boneless chicken
  breast, cut into strips
Salt and pepper
½ cup chopped fresh parsley or cilantro

In a large heavy nonreactive saucepan, heat oil over medium-high heat. Sauté onion, garlic, celery, carrot, and apple until soft, about 6 minutes. Stir in curry, coriander, cumin, turmeric, if using, and flour. Cook about 2 minutes. Stir in tomatoes and potatoes and cook until bubbly. Add stock and bring to a boil. Reduce heat and simmer, uncovered, 20 minutes. Add chicken pieces and simmer 10 minutes. (Do not let soup boil, or chicken will become tough.) Taste for salt and pepper. Serve garnished with parsley.

Serves 6 to 8

GINGERED GOLDEN BEET SOUP

Made with sun-yellow beets, this golden purée is bright in color and in taste. Baking the beets concentrates the sugar and intensifies the sweetness, but the soup's complex tastes really emerge with the addition of fresh ginger and balsamic vinegar. If you make this soup with red beets so that it looks like borscht, its gingery flavor will come as a delightful surprise.

---

8 medium golden beets
½-inch piece fresh ginger, peeled
2 cups Chicken Stock (page 20) or Vegetable
   Stock (page 25)
1 tablespoon balsamic vinegar
2 tablespoons low-fat sour cream
Salt and pepper
2 tablespoons chopped fresh parsley
4 tablespoons chopped chives

Preheat the oven to 375 degrees F. Trim the beets of greens and roots. Wrap each beet in aluminum foil and bake until easily pierced with tip of a knife, about 45 minutes. When cool enough to handle, peel beets. Julienne or shred 2 beets and set aside. Cut remaining beets into 1-inch cubes.

In a blender or food processor, purée cubed beets with ginger, stock, and vinegar. Pour into a medium pot and simmer about 10 minutes. Stir in reserved shredded beets. Whisk in sour cream until well blended. Taste for salt and pepper. Sprinkle with parsley and chives and serve.

Serves 6

CELERY AND ROQUEFORT SOUP

The dieter's standby, celery, is usually consumed raw and mostly eaten instead—instead of potato chips, instead of pretzels, instead of cashews, instead of all those predinner nibbles everyone else seems to be able to feast on without suffering any weighty consequences. But celery has more to offer, especially as a cooked vegetable. In fact, in Louisiana territory, celery is big-time. Along with onion and bell pepper, it is a member of the holy trinity, that trio of ingredients that forms the flavor base of the Cajun and Creole repertoire. In this soup, celery comes into its own, enriched by the very small amount of Roquefort.

---

2 tablespoons vegetable oil
1 large onion, chopped
1 leek, white part only, thoroughly washed
  and chopped
1 medium head celery with lots of leaves, chopped
2 tablespoons flour
4 cups Chicken Stock (page 20)
2 ounces Roquefort cheese or good quality
  blue cheese
Salt and pepper
2 tablespoons celery seed

In a large heavy saucepan, heat oil over medium-high heat. Cook onion, leek, and celery, covered, until soft, about 12 minutes. Stir in flour and cook another minute or so. Stir in stock and cook until slightly thickened, about 3 minutes. Cover and simmer about 35 minutes. In a blender or food processor purée mixture. Return to pot. Mash cheese with a little soup and whisk into hot soup. Taste for salt and pepper. Serve sprinkled with celery seed.

Serves 6

Lentils may be the heart of this soup, but its character depends on the two faces of chard. A member of the beet family, chard gives us firm crisp stems to pick up the flavors of the surrounding vegetables plus shiny ruffled leaves, which brighten each bowlful at the end.

---

2 tablespoons olive oil
1 medium onion, chopped
2 cloves garlic, chopped
1 bunch chard, about 8 ounces, stems sliced
  and leaves cut into thin strips
1 tablespoon cumin seeds, toasted (page 31)
  and crushed
½ teaspoon ground coriander
1½ cups lentils
2 cups chopped tomatoes
¼ cup tomato paste
4 cups water
¼ cup fresh lemon juice
Salt and pepper

In a large heavy nonreactive pot, heat oil over medium-high heat. Cook onion, garlic, and chard stems until wilted, about 5 minutes. Stir in cumin, coriander, and lentils and cook another minute until fragrant. Add tomatoes, tomato paste, and water and bring to a boil. Reduce heat and simmer 30 minutes. Add chard leaves and simmer another 5 minutes. Remove from heat and stir in lemon juice. Taste for salt and pepper and serve.

Serves 6 to 8

CHICK PEA AND ARUGULA SOUP WITH GARLIC AND MINT

Nothing could be easier to make than this busy-day soup, which takes only seconds to put together. The nutty flavors of arugula and creamy chick peas make it an especially earthy delight.

---

2 cups cooked chick peas, fresh or canned
2 cloves garlic
4 tablespoons olive oil
2 tablespoons fresh lemon juice
¼ teaspoon cayenne
4 cups Chicken Stock (page 20) or water or
  a mixture
1 bunch (6 ounces) arugula, coarsely chopped
2 tablespoons chopped fresh mint
3 tablespoons chopped fresh parsley
Salt and pepper

In a blender or food processor, purée chick peas, garlic, olive oil, lemon juice, cayenne, and stock. In a medium pot, cook the arugula over medium heat, just until it begins to wilt. Pour chick pea purée into pot and cook until heated through. Stir in half the mint and parsley. Taste for salt and pepper. Serve, garnished with remaining mint and parsley.

Serves 4 to 6

RED PEPPER AND PINTO PURÉE

Undoubtedly the pinto bean's most famous role is *frijoles refritos* (refried beans). Although this brown speckled bean is a favorite in many Latin American and Mexican dishes, the United States produces more pintos—between seven and fourteen billion pounds yearly—than any other dried bean. Full of B vitamins, calcium, iron, and phosphorus, the pinto also includes complex carbohydrates, which break down slowly. This pepper-red purée is both pretty and satisfying, even in small portions.

---

2 tablespoons olive oil
1 sweet onion, chopped
6 large red bell peppers, seeded and chopped
½ teaspoon salt
⅛ teaspoon cayenne
5 cups Chicken Stock (page 20) or
  Vegetable Stock (page 25)
2 cups cooked pinto beans
3 tablespoons sherry vinegar
½ cup chopped chives

In a large heavy saucepan, heat oil over medium-high heat. Cook onion and peppers until soft, about 8 minutes. Add salt, cayenne, and stock. Bring to a boil, reduce heat, and simmer, uncovered 15 minutes. Add 1 cup beans and simmer another 10 minutes. Purée mixture in a food processor or blender with vinegar. Return to pot and stir in remaining beans. Heat through if necessary. Serve sprinkled with chives.

Serves 8

PEA AND PARSNIP SOUP

With dried peas as a thickener, this chervil-scented parsnip purée provides a full-bodied hearty dish with a hint of sweetness. The fresh peas add an opulent crowning touch.

---

2 tablespoons olive oil
¼ cup chopped shallots
1 leek, white part only, thoroughly
  washed and chopped
1 stalk celery, sliced
4 parsnips, peeled and sliced
½ cup green or yellow split peas
4 cups Chicken Stock (page 20) or
  Vegetable Stock (page 25)
½ cup fresh chervil or parsley leaves
2 cups peas, fresh or frozen
Salt and pepper

In a large heavy saucepan, heat oil over medium-high heat. Cook shallots, leek, and celery until soft, about 8 minutes. Add parsnips, split peas, and stock. Bring to a boil, reduce heat, and simmer, 45 minutes. Purée with half the chervil in a blender or food processor. Return to pot and add peas. Cook on low heat about 6 minutes. Taste for salt and pepper. Serve garnished with remaining chervil.

Serves 6

TOMATO-MUSHROOM BISQUE

This wonderful dish can taste completely different each time you make it, depending on your choice of mushrooms. The amazing thing is that anything works, from morels and matsutakes to chanterelles and ordinary corner-grocery buttons. Thickened with bread crumbs and tinged with tarragon, this bisque offers body and flavor with minimal calories.

---

2 tablespoons olive oil
¾ pound mushrooms, sliced
1 small onion, chopped
1 clove garlic, chopped
1 cup fresh bread crumbs
3 cups tomatoes, seeded and chopped
1 tablespoon tomato paste
2 teaspoons fresh tarragon or ½ teaspoon
   dried tarragon
3 cups Chicken Stock (page 20) or
   Vegetable Stock (page 25)
Salt and pepper

In a large heavy nonreactive saucepan, heat oil over medium-high heat. Cook mushrooms until brown around edges, about 10 minutes. Remove half with a slotted spoon and set aside. Add onion and garlic to mushrooms in pan and cook until soft, about 5 minutes. Stir in bread crumbs, tomatoes, tomato paste, and tarragon. Cook until bubbly. Add stock and bring to a boil. Reduce heat and simmer, uncovered, 20 minutes. Purée in a blender or food processor. Reheat with reserved mushrooms. Taste for salt and pepper and serve.

Serves 6 to 8

NOTES

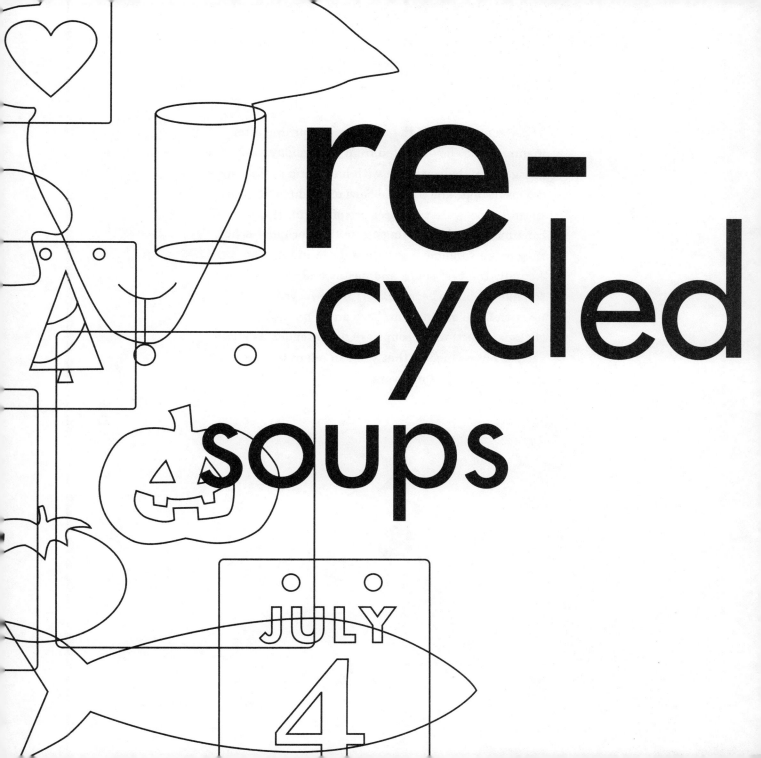

These soups fall into the category of morning-after inspirations. They resulted from postholiday sweeps of refrigerator shelves laden with half a cup of this, six scoops of that, and a whole bowl of crudités. Because these Tupperware treasures are often full of condiments and seasonings from their original debut, they make valuable beginnings for brand new soups. Actually the best soups and pastas and risottos and the like probably began as fortunate recyclings spiffed up with fresh sprigs of an herb and a crumble of cheese. In fact, these soups are not intended as strict recipes but as models that you can adapt to your particular array of leftovers.

"Please finish the salad or I'll have to throw it out. It won't be any good tomorrow." Thus have so many Caesars and Waldorfs met their final demise. Overly productive salad makers will therefore welcome this soup, which puts all but the most wilted greens in a mélange both delicious and ecologically correct.

---

4 cups leftover Caesar salad
2 large tomatoes, seeded and coarsely chopped
1 cup Chicken Stock (page 20) or Vegetable
  Stock (page 25)
Salt and pepper
¼ cup chopped fresh basil or parsley

In a medium bowl, combine the salad, tomatoes, and stock. Let sit at room temperature about 1 hour. In a food processor or blender, process to desired consistency. (We like it just short of smooth.) Taste for salt and pepper. Sprinkle with basil or parsley. May be served chilled, room temperature, or warmed through.

Serves 6

STEAK AND POTATO VEGETABLE SOUP

Like the weather, everyone talks about grilling outdoors, but we don't do anything about it as often as we'd like. When we finally do, we tend to overdo, to assure that everyone gets just what he or she likes. This is a soup for the following day, the cookout transformed.

---

2 tablespoons oil
1 large onion, thinly sliced
1 red bell pepper, seeded and thinly sliced
2 teaspoons Worcestershire sauce
2 cups cooked steak strips
6 cups Beef Stock (page 21) or Chicken
  Stock (page 20)
1 cup shelled peas, fresh or frozen
2 cups scrubbed, diced, and cooked potatoes
Salt and pepper

In a large heavy pot, heat oil over medium-high heat. Cook onion and pepper until soft, about 5 minutes. Stir in Worcestershire sauce and steak. Cook another minute. Add stock, bring to a boil, and add peas and potatoes. Reduce heat and simmer until heated through, about 3 minutes. Taste for salt and pepper and serve.

Serves 6

FRUIT SALAD SOUP

This versatile fruit soup, which uses any seasonal fresh fruits, is a treat any time of the year. With its aromatic spices and tang of balsamic vinegar, it makes a refreshing first course, dessert, or lunch.

---

3 cups leftover fruit salad
½ to 1 cup sugar, or to taste
1 teaspoon ground coriander
½ teaspoon ground cumin
3 tablespoons balsamic vinegar
1 teaspoon grated orange zest
1 teaspoon grated lemon zest
3 cups yogurt
Mint leaves

In a blender or food processor, purée fruit salad, sugar, coriander, cumin, vinegar, and both zests. Pour into a bowl and stir in yogurt until well blended. Cover and chill overnight. Serve garnished with mint.

Serves 6

GRILLED HOT DOG AND SAUERKRAUT SOUP

We think of this as Newlyweds Soup because is was inspired by a collection of easy recipes assembled for couples with little or no cooking experience. Actually this recipe, with its popping mustard seeds, is far more sophisticated. Still, it remains quite an accessible treat and a great way to get kids interested in cooking.

---

2 tablespoons oil
1 large red onion, thinly sliced
1 tablespoon brown sugar
1 tablespoon mustard seed
1 cup sauerkraut, drained
4 cooked hot dogs, sliced
5 cups Beef Stock (page 21) or Chicken Stock
   (page 20)
Salt and pepper
Pickle relish (optional)

In a medium pot, heat oil over medium-high heat. Cook onion until soft, about 4 minutes. Stir in brown sugar and mustard seed. Cook until mustard seeds pop, about 2 minutes. Add sauerkraut and hot dogs and stock. Simmer 5 minutes. Taste for salt and pepper. Garnish with pickel relish, if desired.

Serves 6

Occasionally, even if you hate the word toothsome, it comes to mind with soups like this. The wild rice is mostly to blame because of its earthy, nourishing nature. The full cup of watercress contributes newness to the pot and gives the dish its characteristic zip.

---

2 tablespoons oil
4 scallions, trimmed and thinly sliced
½ cup chopped tomatoes
3 fresh sage leaves chopped or
   ½ teaspoon dried sage
2 cups diced cooked chicken or other poultry
1 cup cooked wild rice
6 cups Chicken Stock (page 20)
1 cup watercress leaves, coarsely chopped

In a medium saucepan, heat oil over medium-high heat. Cook scallions until soft, about 4 minutes. Stir in tomatoes and sage. Cook until bubbly. Add chicken, rice, and stock. Bring to a boil, stir in watercress, and serve.

Serves 6

Salmon garnished with cool sliced cucumbers and dill is a whole spring festival on a plate and the chance of leftovers is slight indeed. But you can use just about any fish here; you can even substitute leftover potatoes, if you have them. And if you have no leftovers at all, this fine and flavorful soup is easy enough to make from scratch and is more than worth the effort.

2 tablespoons oil or butter
4 scallions, trimmed and chopped
1 stalk celery, chopped
⅛ teaspoon cayenne
2 tablespoons flour
3 cups Chicken Stock (page 20) or water
1 large all-purpose potato, peeled and diced
1 cup milk
2 cups flaked cooked salmon
1 medium hothouse cucumber, peeled, seeded,
    halved lengthwise, and sliced
Salt and pepper
3 tablespoons chopped fresh dill

In a large saucepan, heat oil over medium-high heat. Cook scallions and celery until soft, about 5 minutes. Stir in cayenne and flour. Cook, stirring, about 1 minute. Stir in stock gradually and bring to a boil. Soup will thicken a little. Add potato and simmer 15 minutes. In a food processor or blender, purée a ladleful of soup mixture with milk. Return to pot. Add salmon and cucumber. Heat gently about 5 minutes. Taste for salt and pepper. Serve garnished with dill.

Serves 4

La cucina povera is the Italian phrase for the peasant cookery that underlies so many of Italy's beloved dishes. This soup comes straight out of that tradition, transforming a few stale crusts and little else into a rustic and nourishing lunch or supper.

---

2 tablespoons butter or oil
4 large onions, sliced
3 cloves garlic, sliced
4 to 5 cups Chicken Stock (page 20) or water
1 loaf, firm-textured, day-old bread, thinly
*   sliced into 24 slices*
2 cups grated sharp cheese, such as cheddar,
*   longhorn, or gouda*
Chopped chives or fresh parsley

In a large heavy saucepan, heat butter over medium heat. Cook onions and garlic until they are very soft and they just begin to turn golden brown, about 10 minutes. Add stock and bring to a boil. Reduce heat and simmer, uncovered, about 25 minutes. Meanwhile, prepare 6 shallow soup plates by placing 2 slices of bread in each, sprinkling bread with cheese, and covering with remaining slices of bread sprinkled with cheese. Ladle onion soup over bread slices. Sprinkle with chives and serve.

Serves 6

The minute you serve this unusual soup, the lightly crusted triangles of risotto slowly begin to melt into the flavorful stock surrounding them. Once you taste this phenomenon, you'll always want to cook a little extra risotto so you'll have enough to make this dish again.

---

2 cups leftover risotto
1 egg, lightly beaten
¼ cup grated cheese
3 tablespoons butter or oil
6 cups Chicken Stock (page 20)
2 cups peas or other leftover vegetable
2 tablespoons chopped fresh parsley

In a medium bowl, combine risotto with egg and cheese.

In an 8-inch skillet heat butter over medium heat. Spread risotto in skillet and cook until golden brown, about 3 minutes per side. Let cool and cut into 6 wedges. Heat stock with peas. Place a risotto wedge in each of 6 soup plates. Ladle hot stock and peas over risotto. Sprinkle with parsley and serve.

Serves 6

We're tempted to call this soup *seis de mayo* (the sixth of May) because it's a perfect way to use up any feast day leftovers from the Mexican holiday, Cinco de Mayo. The soup is a boon for a larder of leftover, brittling tortillas and even slightly stale cheese. The fresh cilantro at the end covers a multitude of leftovers.

---

8 day-old tortillas, halved and cut into
  1-inch-wide strips
3 tablespoons butter
¼ cup chopped shallots
1 red bell pepper, seeded and chopped
1 or 2 small hot chili peppers, seeded
  and chopped
3 tablespoons flour

½ teaspoon ground cumin
½ teaspoon ground coriander
4 cups Chicken Stock (page 20)
2 cups milk
2 cups shredded flavorful cheese such as
  cheddar, jack, Muenster, Gouda, or a mixture
Salt and pepper
½ cup fresh cilantro leaves

Preheat oven to 375 degrees F. Place tortilla strips on a baking sheet and bake until crisp, about 10 minutes. Set aside to cool.

In a large pot, heat butter over medium heat. Cook shallots and peppers until soft, about 5 minutes. Stir in flour, cumin, and coriander and cook another 2 minutes. Gradually stir in stock and bring to a boil. Reduce heat and simmer, covered, 10 minutes. Add milk, bring to a boil, and gradually stir in cheese, half a cup at a time, stirring to melt each batch before adding more. Taste for salt and pepper. Divide tortilla strips among 8 soup bowls. Ladle soup over them and garnish with cilantro.

Serves 8

HAM, ASPARAGUS, AND WHITE BEAN SOUP

Our rickety old *Joy of Cooking,* with its wobbly cover and splattered pages, provides our favorite definition of eternity: two people and a ham. No matter how many people you invite to share the Easter ham, the leftovers loom large on the refrigerator shelf for days to come. This soup can make the time go by more deliciously.

2 tablespoons oil
1 onion, chopped
1 celery stalk, chopped
1 carrot, chopped
1 tablespoon fresh tarragon leaves or
   ½ teaspoon dried tarragon
6 cups Chicken Stock (page 20)
2 cups diced cooked ham
2 cups cooked asparagus,
   cut into 1-inch pieces
1 cup cooked small white beans
Salt and pepper

In a large heavy pot, heat oil over medium-high heat. Cook onion, celery, and carrot until soft, about 6 minutes. Stir in tarragon and stock. Bring to a boil and add ham, asparagus, and beans. Simmer 5 minutes. Taste for salt and pepper and serve.

Serves 6

This is definitely a lazy-summer-day dish, adaptable to just about any holiday leftovers. A few independent thinkers we know have actually made this soup deliberately *on* the actual holiday. No one was overly horrified at this revolutionary gesture; in fact no one could get enough of this tasty meal-in-a-bowl, which is at once familiar and different.

---

4 cups diced grilled vegetables, such as
  eggplant, zucchini, red peppers, potatoes,
  and onions
2 grilled or fresh tomatoes, seeded
  and chopped
3 cups Chicken Stock (page 20)
2 cups cooked corn kernels
2 cups crumbled cooked hamburger
Salt and pepper

In a blender or food processor, purée vegetables and tomatoes. Place in a large nonreactive pot with stock and stir well to blend. Simmer 10 minutes and add corn and hamburger. Simmer another 5 minutes. Taste for salt and pepper and serve.

Serves 6

APPLE AND PUMPKIN SOUP

Bobbing for apples requires only one ingredient—apples!—and lots of them. Chances are, you'll still have lots of them when the bobbers have finished bobbing and the trick-or-treaters have been by. Along with the too-prevalent pumpkins—not the one you used for the jack-o'-lantern, of course—they make a great warming and spicy soup.

---

4 cups Chicken Stock (page 20)
4 apples, peeled, cored, and diced
2 cups diced pumpkin
1 small onion, diced
½ teaspoon ground cinnamon
½ teaspoon freshly grated nutmeg
½ teaspoon ground coriander
1 cup apple cider
½ cup sour cream
Salt and pepper
¼ cup chopped chives

In a large nonreactive pot, bring stock to a boil. Add apples, pumpkin, onion, cinnamon, nutmeg, and coriander. Simmer, partly covered, 30 minutes. Purée mixture in a food processor or blender. Return to pot. In a small bowl, whisk together cider and sour cream until smooth. Stir into soup mixture and reheat gently. Taste for salt and pepper. Sprinkle with chives and serve.

Serves 6 to 8

By the weekend after Thanksgiving, there's probably not enough turkey left for thick sandwich-size slices, but there's usually plenty to dice up for a soup. A few new noodles tossed in with just about any mix of last Thursday's vegetables and you've magically created an effortless weekend meal.

---

6 cups Turkey Stock or Chicken
    Stock (page 20)
8 ounces wide egg noodles,
    broken into 2-inch lengths
2 cups leftover green vegetables, such as
    brussels sprouts or green beans
2 cups diced, cooked turkey or chicken
1 medium tomato, seeded and chopped
¼ cup chopped fresh parsley
Salt and pepper

In a large nonreactive saucepan, bring stock to a boil. Add noodles and simmer 5 minutes. Stir in vegetables, turkey, and tomato. Cook another 5 minutes. Stir in parsley, taste for salt and pepper, and serve.

Serves 6

CRANBERRY AND CARROT BORSCHT

Because of their high acid content, cranberries keep practically forever in the refrigerator, not to mention the freezer. Even so, they practically disappear by the first of the year after two major doses of these crimson-colored cousins of the blueberry. This berried borscht has become a tangy sweet winter favorite for whatever's left.

---

1 pound carrots, chopped
2 cups cranberries, fresh or frozen
4 cups water or Chicken Stock (page 20)
3 tablespoons sugar or to taste
1 tablespoon fresh lemon juice
½ cup sour cream
2 tablespoons chopped fresh dill

In a medium nonreactive saucepan, simmer carrots, cranberries, stock, and sugar until carrots are very tender, about 20 minutes. In a blender or food processor, purée mixture and return to pan. Add lemon juice. Whisk in sour cream until well blended. Serve garnished with dill.

Serves 6

NOTES

NOTES

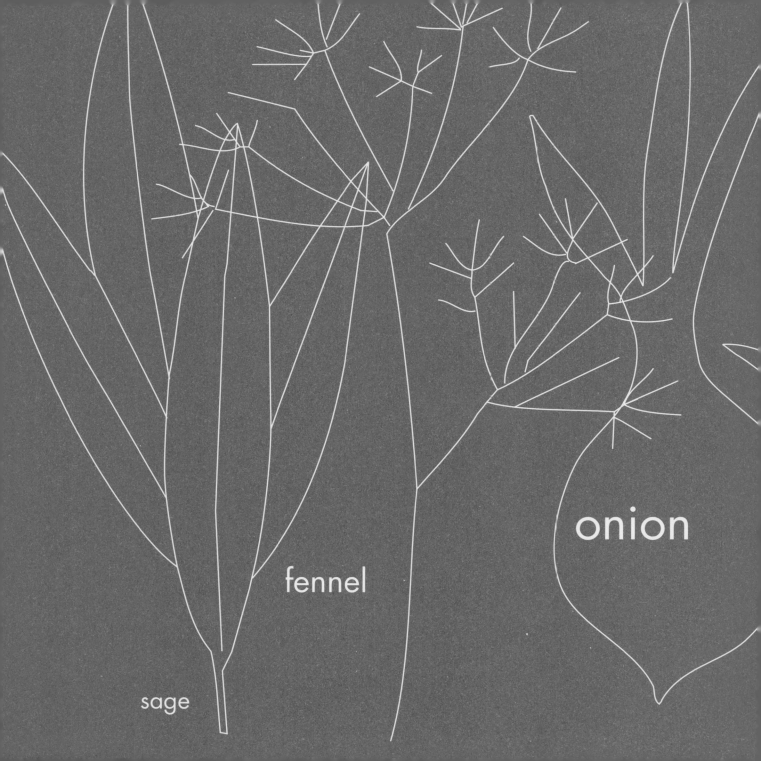

sage

fennel

onion

Like grand old movie stars, these folksoups are the celebrities of soupdom. Many have been around for centuries, delighting and tantalizing all who seek out their charms. Because their specific origins are usually shrouded in mystery, they have a fascination and mystique that makes us want to know more about them. But their stories, from goulash to minestrone, bouillabaisse to cock-a-leekie, are too ancient and myth-bound, too spiced with spirit and pride; in a sense, they offer their heritage and history in the microcosm of the soup pot. Their flavors are as rich and full as the cultures that spawned them; they are past and future, continuity and hope.

We've found that the best accompaniment for these great dishes is to tell your guests the story of their backgrounds, which we provide preceding each recipe. Somehow it makes everything taste more important.

Pistou is more than a Niçoise version of Genoese pesto. It is evidence that the Genoese spent some important time on the French Riviera. It is also a lesson in Italian-French taste preferences. Italians prefer the aggressive pungency of their version, which they use as a sauce with pasta and vegetables as well as a flavoring for soup. The French insist that their basil-and-tomato-based pistou is more subtle and refined; they use it only as a flavoring to stir into pistou soup. Both agree, however, that the basil sauce is not cooked with the soup but added just before serving, either stirred in or as a dollop in each bowl, as we suggest. Ours is a bit of a compromise, as we add pine nuts to the sauce and sundried tomatoes to both the pistou and the minestrone-style soup.

SOUP

6 cups water

2 carrots, halved lengthwise and thinly sliced

1 stalk celery, thinly sliced

*1 leek, white part only, thoroughly washed
  and chopped*

1 large baking potato, peeled and diced

*½ cup dry or oil-packed sundried
  tomatoes, chopped*

1 medium turnip, diced

*½ pound green beans, trimmed and cut
  into ½-inch pieces*

1 cup cooked small white beans

½ cup ditalini pasta or other small pasta

Salt and pepper

PISTOU

3 cloves garlic, peeled

4 tablespoons pine nuts, toasted (page 31)

2 cups fresh basil leaves

6 sundried tomatoes, dry or oil-packed

½ teaspoon thyme

½ cup grated Parmesan cheese

⅓ cup olive oil

Salt and pepper

To make the pistou, combine all ingredients in a food processor or blender and process until a rough paste is formed. Taste for salt and pepper. May be stored in refrigerator about 1 week.

To make soup, in a large nonreactive pot bring the water to a boil. Add carrots, celery, leek, potato, tomatoes, and turnip and simmer 30 minutes. Add green beans, white beans, and pasta and simmer another 10 minutes. Taste for salt and pepper. Place a tablespoon or so of pistou in each soup bowl. Ladle soup over pistou.

Serves 8

POTAGE SAINT-GERMAIN

Despite its fanciful name, this is a very economical soup in France. The famous French chef, Louis Diat, reported that in his family, they not only cooked the pods as well as the peas, they also prepared the soup the day after they had leeks so they could use the leftover green parts of the vegetable in the soup.

Although the soup itself was actually developed in the town of Saint-Cloud near Paris, it was named in honor of the neighboring Saint-Germain, which once produced the most exceptional peas in the country. Ours is a new rendition of the classic, with nice texture from barely cooked snow peas.

6 slices bacon
2 cups peas, fresh or frozen
1 sprig fresh thyme or ½ teaspoon
   dried thyme
6 cups water or Chicken Stock (page 20)
½ pound Sugar Snap peas, strings removed,
   cut into 1-inch pieces
Salt and pepper

Cook bacon until crisp. Crumble and set aside. Place peas, thyme, and the water in a large heavy pot. Bring to a boil and simmer until peas are tender, about 20 minutes. Purée in a blender or food processor. Return to pot with Sugar Snap peas. Simmer 5 minutes. Taste for salt and pepper. Serve sprinkled with crumbled bacon.

Serves 6

POT AU FEU

"The pot must smile"—so goes the ancient French kitchen wisdom. For Pot au Feu, this translates into slow cooking of several good vegetables plus a mixture of meats. The specific ingredients depend on the region, but nothing with any flavor left in it is out of the question. "An old pigeon...a crow in November or December, add greatly to the flavor and aroma..." directs Alexandre Dumas in his *Dictionary of Cuisine*. The essence of the dish is that it produces a two-course meal: The first is the strained bouillon served with pasta, rice, or toasted bread; next come the meat and vegetables, served with such garnishes as those we suggest.

---

3 tablespoons vegetable oil

*2 pounds chicken breasts, skinned and cut
  into pieces*

*1 pound smoked duck sausage, cut into 1-inch
  slices*

3 pounds beef stew meat

2 pounds beef or lamb short ribs

3 cloves garlic, thinly sliced

¼ cup chopped fresh parsley

3 cups Riesling wine

*6 cups Chicken Stock (page 20) or Beef Stock
  (page 21)*

3 cups water

18 baby carrots

18 small white boiling onions, peeled

2 parsnips, peeled and cut into 1-inch pieces

2 stalks celery, cut into 2-inch pieces

6 small turnips

18 small red new potatoes, scrubbed

Salt and pepper

ACCOMPANIMENTS

Horseradish

Mustard

Cornichons

In a large heavy pot, heat oil over medium-high heat. Brown chicken breast, remove, and set aside. Brown sausage, remove, and set aside. Brown beef and short ribs. Add garlic, parsley, and wine and bring to a boil. Reduce heat and simmer about 10 minutes. Add stock and water, bring to a boil, and reduce to a simmer. Skim off any foam that forms on surface, cover, and simmer 2 hours. Add reserved chicken and sausage, carrots, onions, parsnips, celery, turnips, and potatoes. Simmer until all vegetables are tender, about 30 minutes.

Remove meats and vegetables from broth and arrange on platter. Strain broth through a fine-mesh strainer and return to pot over low heat. Taste for salt and pepper and spoon some broth over meats and vegetables. Pot au Feu may be served in 2 courses: first, the broth with noodles or rice; second, the meats and vegetables with horseradish, mustard, and cornichons as accompaniments.

Serves 6

Like a less flashy, unidentical twin, Bourride is often compared invidiously with bouillabaisse, the masterpiece of Marseilles. Yet some of the world's most famous tastebuds have actually favored Bourride; Elizabeth David wrote of it "... this is perhaps the best fish dish of Provence, to my taste much superior to the Bouillabaisse." Characteristic is the garlic mayonnaise, or aïoli, that is both stirred into the soup and spread on the toasts. Some authorities say that Bourride should contain only white fish, never shellfish, and that saffron is never included in its ingredients. On the other hand, *Larousse Gastronomique* lists saffron in its recipe. We've committed a few unorthodoxies of our own, such as puréeing the soup, but the result retains the spirit of the dish.

SOUP
2 tablespoons olive oil
1 onion, chopped
1 small fennel bulb, trimmed, cored,
  and chopped
3 pounds assorted white fish fillets, cut
  into chunks
1 sprig fresh thyme or ½ teaspoon
  dried thyme
1 bay leaf
6 to 7 cups water
Salt and pepper

GARLIC MAYONNAISE
4 cloves garlic, peeled
¼ teaspoon salt
1 egg yolk at room temperature
2 tablespoons fresh lemon juice
1½ cups olive oil

16 slices baguette, toasted

To make the mayonnaise, in a food processor or blender, purée garlic, salt, egg yolk, and lemon juice. With machine running, slowly pour in olive oil until you have a mayonnaise. Set aside.

To make the soup, in a heavy medium pot, heat oil over medium-high heat. Cook onion and fennel until soft, about 6 minutes. Add fish, thyme, bay leaf, and water and bring to a boil. Reduce heat and simmer 10 minutes. Remove fish and about 2 cups liquid to food processor (or in batches, to a blender) and purée. Stir in ½ cup garlic mayonnaise. Return fish purée to pot with remaining liquid and stir well to combine. Taste for salt and pepper. Spread remaining garlic mayonnaise on toasts. Ladle soup into bowl and float toasts on top or pass bowl of garlic mayonnaise for stirring directly into soup. Serve hot.

Serves 6 to 8

Fish soup is fish soup, but Bouillabaisse is Marseilles. Marseilles, where the age-bleached wood of Old Port moans under the wet slap of thick hemp fish-nets, and where a trio of just-caught *rascasse,* their pink-orange scales the same color as the afternoon sun, tries to wriggle away across the dock, unaware that they are the property of the leather-skinned fisherman whose black boots now block their path. Marseilles, where in the kitchens of waterfront restaurants, the chopping of garlic and tomato, the mingling of saffron and olive oil, sound the first notes of the nightly symphony of the Bouillabaisse; and where the baker jumps back from an expected red-devil spark that leaps from his cavernous oven as he lifts out the loaves of *marette,* the special bread to be sliced and submerged in the broth of the Bouillabaisse.

The proprietors of a hundred lopsided brasseries on the Quai des Belges pull down the yellow ocher Bouillabaisse sets—the wide bowl for the broth, the flat plates for the sea perch, *rascasse,* chapon, and shellfish—as they silently rehearse for the evening tourists the legend of Bouillabaisse.

But which legend? Should they tell the tale that Venus, goddess of love, created the dish and spiced it with soporific saffron to lull her husband Vulcan to sleep so she could steal off for a secret tryst with her lover, Mars?

Should they recite the Méry poem about the abbess of the Marseilles convent who devised Bouillabaisse as a Friday fast-day soup?

Perhaps they should go back over two millennia to the Greeks who founded Marseilles and, along with it, the grand dish which makes up part of its wild and mysterious soul?

No matter, smile the lumpy proprietors. Whichever story, the Bouillabaisse will taste of it and be the better for it.

¼ cup olive oil
1 leek, white part only, thoroughly washed
  and chopped
1 large onion, chopped
2 stalks celery, chopped
3 cups seeded and coarsely chopped tomatoes
6 cloves garlic, minced
¼ teaspoon saffron threads
⅛ teaspoon crushed red pepper flakes
1 bay leaf
½ teaspoon dried thyme
1 cup dry red wine
7 cups Fish Stock (page 24) or water
1 pound red snapper fillet, cut into
  small chunks
1 pound halibut fillet, cut into small chunks
1 pound medium shrimp, shelled and deveined
1 pound mussels, scrubbed

Salt and pepper
18 slices baguette, toasted
½ cup Olivada (page 266)
½ cup Sundried Tomato Pesto (page 267)

In a large heavy nonreactive pot, heat oil over medium-high heat. Sauté leek, onion, and celery until soft, about 5 minutes. Add tomatoes and garlic and cook 5 minutes. Stir in saffron, red pepper, bay leaf, thyme, wine, and stock. Bring to a boil and then simmer, uncovered, 30 minutes. Remove bay leaf and purée soup in a blender or food processor or pass through a food mill. Return to pot and bring to a simmer. Add fish and simmer gently until all mussels open, about 5 minutes. Discard any that remain closed. Taste for salt and pepper. Spread half the toasts with Olivada and half with Sundried Tomato Pesto. Serve with soup.

Serves 6 to 8

Garbure has been called the "glory of Béarn." It is a grand dish with just the right balance of French pretentiousness and earthy wisdom, Gallic flair and domestic economy. There is something awesome about sitting down before a bowl of this soup, which has its own rules, its formidable history, its powers. The process of its creation is like the cycle of life, the stages of man: inevitable in a comforting sort of way.

To be scrupulously authentic, Garbure begins with the root word from which it gets its name: a *garbe,* or cluster of herbs and vegetables which flavor the stock. These might include thyme, cabbage, parsley, garlic. The *garbe* goes into an earthenware pot called a *toupi*—the Bearnaise insist a metal pot will interfere with the delicate interplay of flavors. Ingredients, which may include carrots, potatoes, celery, fava beans, peas, cabbage, must be added in a particular order to prevent over- or under-cooking.

Then comes the *trebuc,* which may be ham, sausage, or, on special occasions, preserved goose or pork.

The serving of Garbure involves its own rituals. Quite often, especially in summer, the broth is served prior to the meat, which is allowed to cool. Each serving is ladled over thin slices of stale or toasted bread covered with a savory spread. After the vegetables have been eaten, the knowledgeable Garbure eater knows it is time to *faire goudale.* Each diner stirs a cup of wine into the remaining broth and drinks it down. Herein lies the real power of Garbure, the ability, in the words of a local proverb, to "keep a coin from the doctor's pocket."

Our version, with all those good wholesome vegetables, will undoubtedly do likewise.

2 tablespoons oil
1 pound smoked duck sausage, sliced
 ¼ inch thick
¼ pound cooked ham, diced
1 medium head cabbage, shredded
1 leek, white part only, thoroughly washed
 and sliced
2 cloves garlic, thinly sliced
2 carrots, sliced 1 inch thick
2 small zucchini, sliced 1 inch thick
½ pound green beans, cut into ½-inch pieces
1 cup peas, fresh or frozen
1 cup shelled fava beans or lima beans
¾ pound red new potatoes, scrubbed
 and quartered
3 sprigs fresh parsley
1 sprig fresh thyme
1 sprig fresh rosemary
2 cups water
Salt and pepper

In a large heavy pot, heat oil over medium-high heat. Cook sausage and ham until lightly browned, about 4 minutes. Remove and set aside. Place remaining ingredients, except for salt and pepper, in pot and bring to a boil. Cover, reduce heat, and simmer about 1 hour. Add reserved sausage and ham. Cook another 5 minutes. Taste for salt and pepper and serve.

Serves 8

Mageritsa is a traditional Greek soup eaten after midnight mass on Easter. Made from the entrails of the lamb to be served for the Sunday feast, it is rich with herbs and is often thickened with a bright-tasting, egg-lemon sauce called Avgolemono. This delicate emulsion is also a soup of its own, possibly deriving from a time when people were ravenous for the eggs of which they had been deprived all during Lent. This queen of all Greek soups, as it has been called, makes a versatile background for a variety of ingredients. With fish, it becomes *psarosoupa avgolemono* (customarily served with generously filled glasses of retsina); with celery, it is *selino avgolemono;* served cold it is called *krya*. In our favorite variation, asparagus adds a note of elegance.

---

4 cups Chicken Stock (page 20)
1 pound thin asparagus, trimmed and cut
  into 1-inch pieces
3 tablespoons Arborio rice
¼ cup fresh lemon juice
2 eggs
Salt and pepper

In a medium saucepan, bring stock to a boil. Add asparagus and cook 3 minutes. Remove asparagus with slotted spoon and set aside. Add rice to simmering stock, cover, and cook until rice is tender, about 15 minutes. In a medium bowl, combine lemon juice and eggs until well blended. Add a ladleful of hot broth to egg mixture in a slow stream, whisking steadily. Whisk this mixture into remaining soup. Add asparagus and heat gently until slightly thickened. Taste for salt and pepper and serve.

Serves 4 to 6

When it comes to health food, nothing beats Chicken Soup with Matzo Balls—at least according to its millions of totally convinced fans. Science has recently put in a good word as well: "There's an aromatic substance in chicken soup, not yet identified, that helps clear your airways." So reports Dr. Marvin Sackner, pulmonary specialist at Miami's Mount Sinai Medical Center.

Recipes for chicken soup may be infinite, but there seem to be only two types of matzo balls: the lead balloons and the feather-light floaters. With their tasty addition of fresh herbs, ours remain a respectful variation on what Joan Nathan honors as "the only truly Jewish dish."

MATZO BALLS

2 eggs

2 tablespoons melted chicken fat, margarine,
  or vegetable oil

4 tablespoons Chicken Stock (page 20)

½ cup matzo meal

¼ teaspoon salt

1 tablespoon each chopped parsley, dill,
  and chives

8 cups Chicken Stock (page 20),
  clarified (page 29)

In a large bowl, beat eggs with chicken fat and stock until well blended. Stir in matzo meal, salt, and herbs. Refrigerate about 1 hour.

Bring a large pot of salted water to a boil. With wet hands, form matzo balls about 1 inch in diameter. Do not compact them. Drop in boiling water. When balls float to the surface, turn down to a bare simmer, cover and cook about 35 minutes. Remove with slotted spoon, cover, and refrigerate until ready to use. To serve, heat chicken stock with matzo balls.

Serves 6

When you discuss personal matters, such as borscht, you can expect to get a lot of free advice. Asked to judge a borscht competition, we sampled over a dozen variations on the theme, from thin magenta consommés to meaty stews. But the cooks who belonged to the borschts were convinced—and convincing—that their particular interpretation was the only true procedure. Such controversies have deep roots, as we learn from Berkeley historian Reginald D. Zelnick, who warns (tongue in cheek) that we not underestimate "the power of borscht as a unifying cultural symbol" of Russian national identity. But our favorite perspective comes from Isaac Bashevis Singer quoting his Aunt Yntl: "In a pinch I can make from a chicken soup a borscht, but to make from a borscht a chicken soup, this is beyond any cook."

Balsamic vinegar and orange juice give our version a tangy character that most people enjoy; but when you confess the ingredients, don't be surprised if you get a little free advice with the compliments.

---

1 large head cabbage, shredded

4 large beets, peeled and sliced

2 large onions, thinly sliced

1 can (28 ounces) tomatoes,
   drained and coarsely chopped

2 quarts water

¼ cup brown sugar

¼ cup balsamic vinegar

¼ cup fresh orange juice

2 teaspoons caraway seed

Salt and pepper

Sour cream

Orange slices

Combine cabbage, beets, onions, and tomatoes in a large heavy nonreactive pot. Add 2 quarts water and simmer 1 hour. Stir in the sugar, vinegar, orange juice, and caraway seed and cook another 15 minutes. Taste for salt and pepper. Serve with a dollop of sour cream topped with an orange slice.

Serves 8

SCHAV

Schav is a soup with many variations, but they all begin with sorrel. (The word *schav* is Polish for sorrel.) The sour lemony taste is especially refreshing on a summer day when a cold soup is the perfect meal. To make it even more of a meal, some schav aficionados serve the soup gazpacho-style, accompanied with bowls of garnishes like scallions, chopped cucumbers, and/or sliced radishes. In Jewish families, the serving of boiled potatoes, either in or alongside the soup, is also customary. We like this tart green mélange as is, or simply accompanied with a good loaf of caraway rye.

---

1 pound chard, leaves chopped and
* stems cut into 1-inch pieces*
1 pound spinach leaves, chopped
½ pound sorrel, chopped
6 scallions, trimmed and chopped
8 cups water
3 eggs
1 cup sour cream
Salt and pepper
¼ cup chopped fresh dill or parsley

In a large heavy pot, combine chard, spinach, sorrel, scallions, and the water and bring to a boil. Reduce heat and simmer for 20 minutes. In a food processor or blender combine the eggs and sour cream. Process this mixture with about 2 ladlefuls of soup. Return to pot and stir well. Taste for salt and pepper. Serve hot or let cool, cover, refrigerate, and serve cold. Garnish with dill or parsley before serving.

Serves 8

Like many old peasant dishes, goulash is a creation of circumstance. Its first chefs were the Magyar nomads wandering the lonely Hungarian plains. They got their main ingredient and their shopping bag from the same source. The meat of lamb was dried in the sun on sheepskin, then wrapped and carried until mealtime. This campsite cuisine eventually developed into the national dish of Hungary. The legendary chef and restaurateur, Károly Gundel, once explained, "Most foreigners call all dishes that contain paprika *gulyás*. We Hungarians divide paprika dishes into four varieties: *gulyás, pörkölt, tokány,* and *paprikás."* Our version, with its caraway and paprika, doesn't stray too far from strict authenticity—except, of course, for the sheepskin.

---

3 tablespoons oil
2 medium onions, thinly sliced
2 cloves garlic, minced
⅛ teaspoon cayenne
1 tablespoon sweet Hungarian paprika
1 tablespoon caraway seed

1 green bell pepper, seeded and thinly sliced
1 red bell pepper, seeded and thinly sliced
2 pounds lamb shoulder, cut into 1-inch cubes
3 tablespoons tomato paste
8 cups Beef Stock (page 21)
Salt and pepper

In a large heavy pot, heat oil over medium-high heat. Cook onions and garlic until soft, about 5 minutes. Stir in cayenne, paprika, caraway, and bell peppers. Cook until peppers become soft, about 6 minutes. Add lamb and cook, stirring, until it loses its raw color. Stir in tomato paste and stock. Bring to a boil, turn down to a simmer, and cook until lamb is tender, about 1 hour. Taste for salt and pepper and serve.

Serves 8

HUNGARIAN SOUR CHERRY SOUP

Fortunately for cherry fans, *meggyleves* (cold sour cherry soup) is more difficult to pronounce than to make. This Hungarian classic, in which the tart-sweet fruit is balanced with the heady spice of cinnamon, is the essence of early summer. Some recipes intensify the cherriness by boiling crushed cherry pits in the wine used to make the soup. We simply stir the dried cherries into the hot soup after cooking. This soup is especially wonderful as a chilled counterpoint to any hot or highly spiced course.

---

1 pound sour cherries, pitted, or
  1 can (16 ounces) pitted sour
  cherries, drained
1½ cups water
1½ cups white wine, such as Riesling
¼ cup brown sugar
1 teaspoon ground cinnamon
2 tablespoons fresh lemon juice

3 tablespoons fresh orange juice
2 tablespoons kirsch
2 cups yogurt
1 cup pitted dried cherries
Grated zest of 1 lemon
Grated zest of 1 orange

Combine sour cherries, water, wine, sugar, and cinnamon in a medium nonreactive pot and bring to a boil. Reduce heat and simmer 20 minutes. Stir in lemon and orange juice and kirsch. Let cool. Purée in a blender or food processor and pour into serving bowl. Whisk in yogurt and dried cherries until well blended. Cover, refrigerate, and serve chilled, garnished with lemon and orange zest.

Serves 8

Many peoples, from Armenian and Greek to Indian and Iranian, make yogurt soup, but Bulgarians claim only in their mountain air does milk curdle properly to produce great yogurt. In fact, they insist that the milk should be from water buffalo or goats, whose milk has more butterfat than cows, for proper richness. Their famous Tarator can be traced back to Bulgaria's occupation by the Ottoman Turks, who first planted the walnuts that make this cucumber soup so distinctive. We've toasted the nuts and added some zucchini and basil for an extra jolt of summer, the perfect time for this refreshing cold dish.

---

1 large cucumber, peeled, seeded, and
  cut into chunks
1 medium zucchini or yellow summer
  squash, cut into chunks
1 clove garlic
1 cup walnuts, lightly toasted (page 31)
3 fresh mint leaves
6 fresh basil leaves
3 sprigs fresh dill
3 tablespoons fresh lemon juice
1 teaspoon sugar
¼ cup olive oil
½ teaspoon salt
Pinch cayenne
6 cups yogurt

In a food processor or in batches in a blender, combine all ingredients except yogurt until a rough paste forms. Add yogurt and process until well blended. Chill and serve.

Serves 8

MULLIGATAWNY

We have found many delightful old recipes for this eighteenth-century curried soup. One back-to-basics set of directions begins "Divide a calf's head, well cleaned, and a cow's heel, and put them in a saucepan." Another recipe maker reluctantly adds turmeric, though warning that the spice is "an improvement that can be dispensed with." Then in 1856, *Cookery As It Should Be*, an American cookbook by A Practical Housekeeper, presented "the true Oriental recipe" based on what it called "chicken water." Actually mulligatawny means "pepper water" and was made by Indian cooks for the British colonials, who brought it back to England. In our version we have tempered the heat with cubes of mango and strands of shredded coconut.

---

2 tablespoons butter or vegetable oil
1 large onion, chopped
1 stalk celery, chopped
1 carrot, chopped
1 mango, peeled and cubed
¼ cup unsweetened shredded coconut
3 tablespoons flour
1 tablespoon curry powder
½ teaspoon ground cumin

6 cups Chicken Stock (page 20)
1 skinless and boneless whole chicken breast,
  cut into small cubes
½ cup fresh cilantro leaves,
  coarsely chopped
Salt and pepper
Yogurt
Diced mango

In a heavy medium pot, heat the butter over medium heat. Cook onion, celery, and carrot until soft, about 6 minutes. Stir in mango and coconut and cook 2 minutes. Add flour, curry, and cumin and cook, stirring, 3 minutes. Add stock and bring to a boil. Reduce heat and simmer 20 minutes. Purée half the soup mixture in a food processor or blender and return to pot with chicken. Simmer until chicken is cooked, about 12 minutes. Stir in cilantro and taste for salt and pepper. Garnish with yogurt and diced mango.

Serves 8

COCK-A-LEEKIE

For a dish with so few ingredients, this ancient Scottish stewlike soup causes quite a bit of controversy. The proper cooking of the leeks and prunes is a subject of culinary dispute; some recipes, for example, advise serving a few whole prunes in each bowl; others think the prunes should be cooked in the broth but never served at all. A few purists insist that raisins are the only true tradition. Then there's the poultry dilemma: Should it be a roasting chicken, a capon, or, as one recipe asserts, the losing contender of a cockfight which, for some reason, is believed to impart real body to the broth.

---

3 leeks, white part only, thoroughly washed
   and thinly sliced
3 leeks, thoroughly washed and left whole
4 sprigs fresh parsley
8 cups Chicken Stock (page 20) or Beef Stock
   (page 21), or a mixture of both
2 skinless and boneless whole chicken breasts,
   cut into thin strips
½ pound pitted prunes, halved
Salt and pepper

In a large pot, combine sliced leeks, whole leeks, parsley, and stock and bring to a boil. Reduce heat and simmer 1 hour. Remove whole leeks and discard. Add chicken and prunes and simmer 20 minutes. Taste for salt and pepper and serve.

Serves 8

STRACCIATELLA

Like some of Italy's most delicious dishes, Stracciatella contains a minimum of the most basic ingredients. A chopped basil leaf, a grating of Parmesan, an egg, all stirred together and drizzled slowly at the last minute into a simple broth. With a little ambidextrous stirring and pouring, you get the traditional Roman specialty that looks like tattered rags and tastes greater than the sum of its parts. Additions, depending on the region and the cook, might include a dusting of nutmeg, shreds of lemon peel, a handful of chopped fresh spinach, or even a whole spring lamb, the specialty of the Sabine-Rieti region, northeast of Rome, where the resulting soup is called *agnello in guazzetto*. For texture and interest, we like to stir in some fresh seasonal vegetables.

---

2 eggs
2 tablespoons grated Parmesan cheese
1 tablespoon finely chopped basil
¼ teaspoon salt
6 cups Chicken Stock (page 20)
1 small zucchini, finely grated
1 small carrot, finely grated
Salt and pepper

In a small bowl, whisk together eggs, cheese, basil, and salt until well blended. In a medium pot, bring stock to a boil. Pour in egg mixture, stirring gently with a whisk, and simmer about 2 minutes. Add zucchini and carrot and cook another minute. Taste for salt and pepper and serve.

Serves 6

Tuscany is famous for its bean dishes, some with intriguing names like *fagioli all'uccelletto,* meaning "beans cooked like little birds," and especially *fagioli al fiasco,* in which the beans are cooked in a *fiasco,* a flask like one of those straw-bottomed chianti bottles. Our bean dish also has an intriguing nickname: We call it the Pied Piper Potage because of its effect on anyone within kitchen distance. The minute the prosciutto and pancetta begin their savory mingling in the hot olive oil, people start showing up at the stove. Fortunately this is a quickly made version of the old classic with a flavor that is still fabulous.

---

2 tablespoons olive oil
¼ pound pancetta, diced
3 ounces prosciutto, diced
1 small onion, chopped
1 clove garlic, minced
1 stalk celery, chopped
1 cup chopped tomatoes
½ teaspoon dried sage or 1 teaspoon
   fresh sage

8 cups water or Chicken Stock (page 20)
2 cups small elbow macaroni or other small
   shaped pasta
1 cup cooked cranberry beans or
   kidney beans
1 cup cooked cannellini or white beans
Salt and pepper
Fresh sage or parsley
Grated Parmesan cheese

In a large heavy pot, heat the oil over medium-high heat. Cook pancetta and prosciutto just until they become golden, about 4 minutes. Stir in onion, garlic, and celery and cook until soft, about 3 minutes. Add tomatoes and sage and cook until bubbly. Add the water, bring to a boil, and cook 10 minutes. Stir in pasta and beans and cook another 10 minutes. Taste for salt and pepper. Garnish each serving with a sage leaf or two and pass the cheese.

Serves 8

RECIPE FOR Chicken Soup With Matzo Balls

Matzo Balls

2 eggs

2 Tablespoon Chicken Fat or Oleo.

4 T Chicken Stock

½ cup Matzo meal.

½ teaspoon Salt.

1 T each Chopped parsley, dill & chive

8 cup Chicken Stock.

In a Large Bowl, beat egg with Chicken fat & stock until well blended. Stir in Matzo meal, salt & herbs. Refrigerate for 1 hour.

Bring a large pot of salted water to a boil. With wet hands form matzo balls about 1 in by team (Do not compact them) Drop them in boiling water. When balls float to the top turn down to a low simmer. Cover & Cook about 35 min. Remove with slotted spoon. Cover & refrigerate until ready to use. To Serve heat Chicken stock with matzo Balls.

Irene (c)

In many ways, minestrone can be seen as much more than a soup. It could easily be a geography lesson, since the way it is prepared in Italy's different regions reflects the local character and resources. In Genoa, where minestrone is simmered long hours to develop fully and meld the flavors, the most revered single ingredient might be patience. The Abruzzi version usually contains pig's feet or ham, Sardinians may add pig's ears, and a Milanese interpretation contains rice and pesto and is often served cold. Minestrone might also be an Italian lesson: *Minestra* means soup, but with the diminutive suffix, it becomes Minestrina, a broth or light soup. Our own lightened version is decidedly more *-trina* than *-trone*.

---

2 tablespoons olive oil

2 ounces prosciutto, diced

3 scallions, trimmed and sliced

1 clove garlic, minced

½ pound cremini mushrooms, diced

2 small zucchini, diced

½ fennel bulb, trimmed, cored, and diced

4 cups Chicken Stock (page 20) or water

½ cup pastina or other small pasta

1 cup peas, fresh or frozen

¼ cup chopped basil leaves

Salt and pepper

In a heavy medium pot, heat oil over medium-high heat. Cook the prosciutto until golden brown around edges. Stir in the scallions, garlic, and mushrooms and cook about 5 minutes. Add zucchini and fennel and cook another 2 minutes, stirring. Pour in stock, bring to a boil, and add pastina. Cook 2 minutes and add peas and basil. Cook another 3 minutes. Taste for salt and pepper and serve.

Serves 6

Leave it to the Italian to create a delicious dish with little more than a few slices of bread. *Panzanella,* for example, is simply a thick cut of very dry bread dribbled with olive oil and vinegar. Pappa al Pomodoro is bread and tomato soup, often served as a first course and sometimes served cold. Italians called the tomato *pomodoro* (the golden apple) due to the sunny yellow color of the early varieties that the Moors brought to Italy in the sixteenth century. In our literal interpretation, we include yellow tomatoes when we can get them because they are less acidic. But the ordinary red ones work just as well, as long as they are summer ripe. Sundried tomatoes enhance the flavors of this rich tasting, warm-weather treat.

½ pound day-old, good quality, country-style
   Italian bread, sliced
4 tablespoons olive oil
3 cloves garlic, minced
¼ teaspoon crushed red pepper flakes
1 pound mixed ripe yellow and red tomatoes,
   peeled, seeded, and quartered
½ cup sundried tomatoes, cut into strips
4 cups Chicken Stock (page 20)
Salt and pepper
¼ cup basil leaves
Grated Parmesan cheese (optional)

Place bread in a warm oven (about 250 degrees F). and let dry out but not color. This should take about 30 minutes. Cut into 2-inch cubes. In a medium nonreactive pot, heat oil over medium-high heat. Cook garlic and red pepper about 3 minutes. Add fresh tomatoes, sundried tomatoes, and bread and cook, stirring, until the bread absorbs some of the tomatoes. Stir in stock a little at a time until a thick mush forms. Taste for salt and pepper and stir in basil leaves. Simmer about 10 minutes. Pass cheese or sprinkle each serving with cheese if desired.

Serves 4 to 6

PERSIAN WISHING SOUP

According to Najmieh Batmanglij, in her wonderful book *Food of Life*, the Persian word for soup is *ash;* the cook is *ashe-paz*, "soup preparer"; and the kitchen is *ashe-paz khaneh*, "the place where soup is prepared." This provides a clue to the central importance that Persian culture accords soup, which is often shared to seal bonds of friendship and more amorous relationships.

A famous Persian *ash* is wishing soup, an ad-hoc mélange with a peculiarly Persian fairy-tale twist. According to the directions, a person first must decide to make a wish on a certain day and then invite friends to bring a soup ingredient to the wishmaker's house in the morning of the specified day. At noon, everyone returns to share the resulting soup, which somehow helps make the wish come true.

SOUP
2 tablespoons butter or vegetable oil
1 onion, chopped
¼ teaspoon turmeric
¼ teaspoon ground cinnamon
½ cup rice
¼ pound dried apricots, cut into thin strips
½ cup chopped fresh parsley
8 cups Chicken Stock (page 20) or water
1 cup cooked chick peas

Salt and pepper
¼ cup fresh mint leaves

LAMB BALLS
½ pound ground lamb
½ cup pine nuts, toasted (page 31)
½ onion, chopped
½ teaspoon ground cinnamon
¼ teaspoon salt
¼ teaspoon freshly ground pepper

To make the lamb balls, mix all ingredients until well combined. Form into walnut-size balls and set aside.

To make the soup, in a large pot, heat oil over medium-high heat. Cook onion over low heat until golden, about 6 minutes. Stir in turmeric, cinnamon, and rice. Cook rice until translucent, about 3 minutes. Add apricots, parsley, and stock. Bring to a boil and add lamb balls. Reduce heat and simmer about 20 minutes. Add chick peas and cook another 5 minutes. Taste for salt and pepper. Serve garnished with mint leaves.

Serves 8

Some people have theorized that Cioppino is an Americanization of some Italian fish soup; others think it an Italianization of the English "chip in." This richly seasoned seafood stew supposedly originated in San Francisco's Fishermans Wharf, where Italian fisherman each contributed—or "chipped in"—part of their day's catch to a communal cauldron. Whatever its origins, sourdough or any kind of crusty French bread is necessary to guide the tomatoey broth from tureen to tongue.

3 tablespoons olive oil
2 onions, chopped
3 cloves garlic, chopped
2 stalks celery, chopped
1 carrot, chopped
1 red bell pepper, seeded and chopped
4 large tomatoes, seeded and chopped
3 tablespoons tomato paste
½ teaspoon dried oregano
½ teaspoon dried thyme
¼ cup fresh orange juice

¼ cup fresh lemon juice
2 cups Fish Stock (page 24)
1 cup water
2 cups dry red wine
2 pounds snapper, cut into 2-inch chunks
½ pound sea scallops, cut into quarters
½ pound medium shrimp, shelled
    and deveined
1 large Dungeness crab, cracked
16 mussels, scrubbed
Salt and pepper

In a large heavy nonreactive pot, heat the oil over medium-high heat. Cook onions, garlic, celery, carrot, and red pepper until soft. Stir in tomatoes, tomato paste, oregano, thyme, orange juice, lemon juice, fish stock, and water. Bring to a boil and add wine. Stir and bring to a boil. Reduce heat and simmer, covered, 45 minutes. Add fish and shellfish and simmer about 8 minutes. Discard mussels that don't open. Taste for salt and pepper and serve.

Serves 6

VICHYSSOISE

French chef Louis Diat, who is credited as the inventor of Vichyssoise, complained upon his arrival in America that he couldn't find any leeks. His solution, presaging today's enterprising chefs and restaurateurs, was to persuade someone to grow them for him. This was fortuitous both for the grand opening of New York City's Ritz-Carlton Hotel, for which he created the leek and potato purée, and for steel magnate, Charles Schwab, who had the honor of tasting the first spoonful. Although technically American, Vichyssoise has its roots in the Vichy region of France where Diat grew up enjoying its two potato-leek specialties, *potage bonne femme* and *potage parmentier*. In our interpretation, a sweet potato colors the soup a pretty pale pink.

---

2 tablespoons butter or oil
4 leeks, white parts only, thoroughly washed
  and sliced
¼ cup shallots, chopped
1 sweet onion, chopped
4 large baking potatoes, peeled and diced
1 large sweet potato, peeled and diced
5 cups Chicken Stock (page 20) or water
1 cup milk
Salt and pepper
¼ cup chopped chives

In a large heavy pot, heat the butter over medium heat. Cook leeks, shallots, and onion until very soft, about 8 minutes. Stir in baking potato and sweet potato and cook 2 minutes. Add stock, bring to a boil, and reduce heat. Simmer until potatoes are tender, about 20 minutes. Purée soup in a blender until very smooth. Return to pot with milk and reheat gently. Taste for salt and pepper. Garnish with chives and serve.

Serves 6 to 8

PHILADELPHIA PEPPER POT

If the story of Philadelphia Pepper Pot is true, this soup is undoubtedly George Washington's greatest culinary hit. Not that he got out there in the kitchen himself, but he reportedly did order his Pennsylvania Dutch cook to come up with a hearty meal for the Continental Army at Valley Forge. With only tripe and peppercorns in the larder, the cook managed to devise a soup that so delighted General Washington that he ordered the dish named after the cook's hometown. A century later, the soup had become a popular Philadelphia street food, sold from pushcarts to the accompanying cry, "Peppery pot, smokin' hot; makes backs strong, makes lives long." The revolutionary aspect of our pale green version, flecked with red pepper, is the addition of tiny black pepper dumplings. And we've left out the tripe altogether.

---

2 tablespoons vegetable oil
1 red bell pepper, seeded and diced
1 onion, chopped
1 bag (10 ounces) spinach, coarsely chopped
¾ pound kale, coarsely chopped
1 cup fresh parsley, chopped
1 small potato, peeled and diced
4 cups Vegetable Stock (page 25) or water
1 cup milk

½ teaspoon salt
½ teaspoon freshly ground pepper

BLACK PEPPER DUMPLINGS
½ cup solid vegetable shortening
1 cup flour
1 teaspoon baking powder
½ teaspoon freshly ground pepper
½ teaspoon salt

In a large heavy pot, heat oil over medium-high heat. Cook red pepper just until it starts to wilt, about 3 minutes. Remove with a slotted spoon and set aside. In same pot cook onion until soft, about 5 minutes. Add spinach, kale, and parsley and cook until greens begin to wilt, about 3 minutes. Add potato and stock. Bring to a boil and simmer, uncovered, 15 minutes. Purée mixture in a food processor or blender. Return to pot with milk and season with salt and pepper.

To make the dumplings, combine shortening, flour, baking powder, pepper, and salt to make a fairly stiff dough. Form dough into dumplings the size of marbles and drop in a large pot of simmering water. Cook about 8 minutes. Remove with a slotted spoon and set aside until ready to use. To serve, reheat soup if necessary and stir in reserved red pepper and dumplings.

Serves 6

HOT AND SOUR SOUP

In China, soup is an important part of the meal, though the role it plays is quite different from that in Western cuisines. The bowl of soup, often set in the center of the table, serves as a beverage to be sipped and sampled all during the meal, almost as a palate-cleanser between courses. In fact, the conventional expression for an ordinary family meal—*szu-t'sai yi-t'ang*—translates as "four dishes and one soup." The types of soups can vary from the always surprising mix of leftovers called "Wash-the-pot" to the thin rice soups consumed as midnight snacks.

This hot and sour, China-inspired soup, thick with baby bok choy and black mushrooms, is a favorite with guests. A word of caution: If you can't find fresh water chestnuts, don't used canned ones, which often have an off flavor that can ruin the soup. Substitute diced jícama instead.

---

4 dried Chinese black mushrooms
¼ pound lean pork
1 small skinless and boneless whole
  chicken breast
5 cups Chicken Stock (page 20)
1 teaspoon salt
2 baby bok choy, thinly sliced
1 cup fresh water chestnuts, peeled and sliced,
  or ½ cup diced jícama

2 pieces (8 ounces) fresh bean curd
2 tablespoons cornstarch mixed with
  ¼ cup water
1 egg, lightly beaten
1 tablespoon sesame oil
2 tablespoons white wine vinegar
½ teaspoon freshly ground pepper
2 scallions, trimmed and thinly sliced
½ cup fresh cilantro leaves

Soak mushrooms in hot water 30 minutes. Drain, reserving soaking liquid. Cut mushrooms, pork, and chicken into thin strips. Set aside.

In a large pot, combine stock and soaking liquid. Bring to a boil. Add the salt, bok choy, chestnuts, pork, mushrooms, and chicken. Cover, reduce heat, and simmer about 5 minutes. Add bean curd and cook another minute. Stir a little of the hot stock into cornstarch paste and add this mixture to the soup. Cook another 2 minutes. Slowly add egg to soup, stirring gently. Stir in sesame oil, vinegar, and black pepper. Sprinkle with scallions and cilantro and serve.

Serves 6

A trio of men stands outside the tortilla factory in Guadalajara, watching the wheels and pulleys slap out disk after disk of round, perfect tortillas. Their faces betray suspicion, disappointment. They do not like these machine-made tortillas. Something is wrong. Finally they realize what's missing: the taste of a woman's hands.

Tortillas are a sensitive issue, caught in the collective memory that extends back to the Aztecs, who introduced them to the Spanish. The pride of Yucatán is a tortilla soup called *sopa de lima* made from bitter limes. It comes to the table still sizzling from freshly fried tortilla strips. Though it has no limes—tomatillos provide a citrusy tang—our soup tastes just as hearty. We've lightened the original by baking the tortillas instead of frying them.

---

10 small corn tortillas (6 inches)
3 tablespoons corn oil
1 small onion, chopped
2 cloves garlic, minced
2 jalapeño peppers, seeded and cut into strips
1 Anaheim pepper, seeded and chopped
1 red bell pepper, seeded and cut into
  thin strips
2 teaspoons ground cumin
1 teaspoon dried oregano
2 tomatoes, seeded and coarsely chopped
2 tomatillos, husked, seeded, and
  coarsely chopped

2 tablespoons tomato paste
8 cups Chicken Stock (page 20)
2 skinless whole chicken breasts
1 zucchini, diced
4 scallions, trimmed and thinly sliced
3 cups corn kernels, fresh or frozen
  and thawed
Salt and pepper
Chopped cilantro (optional)
Sour cream (optional)
Shredded jack cheese (optional)

Preheat the oven to 350 degrees F. Cut tortillas in half and then into thin strips. Bake until crisp, about 10 minutes. Set aside.

In a large heavy nonreactive pot, heat oil over medium-high heat. Cook onion, garlic, and peppers until soft, about 6 minutes. Stir in cumin, oregano, tomatoes, tomatillos, and tomato paste. Cook 3 minutes. Add stock, bring to a boil, and add chicken breasts. Reduce heat and simmer, covered, 15 minutes. Do not boil or chicken will get tough and stringy. Remove chicken and let cool. Add zucchini, corn, and scallions and simmer another 8 minutes. Remove chicken from bones and shred into thin strips. Add to soup and heat through. Taste for salt and pepper. To serve, place a handful of tortilla strips in each bowl and ladle soup over them. Garnish with sour cream, cilantro, and cheese if desired.

Serves 10

CALLALOO

The Caribbean soup Callaloo has almost as many spellings as recipes: from *calalu* to *caruru*. All refer to its star ingredient, a large-leafed green vegetable, also called elephant's ear. Some have called this soup a microcosm of the Caribbean because it combines the okra of Africa with the salt cod of colder climates. But in the islands, variations abound: Santa Lucia's *callaloo* has spinach and salted beef, whereas *callaloo voodoo* from Scarborough is a meal in itself. Jamaicans call their version pepperpot and wouldn't think of making it without their distinctive addition: a pair of pig's tails soaked overnight. Here we cook a variety of greens, thickened with okra, seasoned and puréed. The addition of coconut milk and crabmeat gives it a tropical touch.

---

2 tablespoons vegetable oil
1 onion, chopped
2 cloves garlic, minced
1 small hot chili pepper, seeded and chopped
¾ pound chard, chopped
¾ pound spinach, coarsely chopped
1 cup arugula leaves, chopped
6 okra, trimmed and sliced
4 cups water
2 cups coconut milk
Salt and pepper
½ pound cooked crabmeat, flaked

In a large heavy pot, heat oil over medium-high heat. Cook onion, garlic, pepper, chard, spinach, and arugula until wilted, about 4 minutes. Add okra and the water and bring to a boil. Reduce heat and simmer 20 minutes. In a blender or food processor, purée mixture. Return to pot with coconut milk. Stir well to blend. Heat through and taste for salt and pepper. Sprinkle with crabmeat and serve.

Serves 8

VATAPÁ

In Bahia, Brazil, there is a saying: If you eat something with pepper in it every day, things that would normally harm you, won't. Perhaps that is why so many Brazilian dishes contain a pinch or two of the spice, and just to be on the safe side, Brazilians usually serve an extra pot of hot peppery salsa in the middle of the table.

A spoonful of one of Brazil's seafood stews—*Vatapá, moqueca, ensopado, abara*—brings you a delicious insight into the country's synthesis of cultures. These dishes combine the dried shrimp and cod introduced by the Portuguese, the dende oil of Africa, South American manioc, and Far East cloves and cinnamon. But Brazil is Brazil: It is virtually impossible to reproduce the experience of its food outside its borders. Our Vatapá provides a hint of the mystery and sensuousness of the great Brazilian seafood stews.

---

3 tablespoons vegetable oil
2 large onions, chopped
2 cloves garlic, chopped
1 habanero pepper, seeded and chopped
2-inch piece of fresh ginger, peeled and sliced
1 cup chopped tomatoes
¼ cup chopped fresh cilantro
2 tablespoons fresh lemon juice
1 can (14 ounces) coconut cream
1½ cups Fish Stock (page 24) or water

½ cup unsweetened grated coconut
½ pound cooked bay shrimp
1½ pounds medium shrimp, shelled
* and deveined*
1½ pounds red snapper, cut into
* 2-inch pieces*
Salt and pepper
1 cup dry-roasted peanuts, coarsely chopped
Fresh cilantro, coarsely chopped

In a large heavy nonreactive pot, heat oil over medium-high heat. Cook onions, garlic, and pepper until soft, about 4 minutes. Stir in ginger, tomatoes, cilantro, lemon juice, coconut cream, fish stock, and grated coconut. Bring to a boil and add bay shrimp. Cook 5 minutes. Purée mixture in a blender or food processor until smooth. Return to pot. If very thick add more water. Simmer and add shrimp and snapper. Cook another 4 minutes. Taste for salt and pepper. Serve with a sprinkling of chopped peanuts and fresh cilantro.

Serves 6

BRAZILIAN BLACK BEAN SOUP

This gutsy soup recalls *feijoada,* Brazil's national dish found throughout the country from Rio to the Amazon. The dish scintillates with its mixture of Portuguese, Indian, and African ingredients. Like *feijoada,* this soup makes a great Saturday dish for a food-loving crowd of friends.

---

1 pound Portuguese linguiça sausage, sliced
2 medium onions, chopped
2 cloves garlic, minced
2 stalks celery, chopped
1 jalapeño pepper, seeded and chopped
¼ cup chopped fresh parsley
1 tablespoon grated orange zest
1 tablespoon grated lemon zest
1 teaspoon ground cumin
4 cups cooked black beans

8 cups Beef Stock (page 21) or water,
*   or a combination*
1 bay leaf
¼ cup sherry or sherry vinegar
¼ cup fresh orange juice
Salt and pepper
2 hard-cooked eggs, chopped
Lemon slices
Orange slices

In a large heavy nonreactive pot, cook sausage until most of fat is rendered and sausage is browned. Remove sausage with a slotted spoon and set aside. Discard all but 3 tablespoons of fat from pot. Sauté onions, garlic, celery, and jalapeño until soft, about 7 minutes. Stir in parsley, orange zest, lemon zest, and cumin. Cook another minute. Add beans, stock, and bay leaf. Bring to a boil and simmer, partly covered, about 1 hour. Purée in a blender or food processor. Return to pot and stir in reserved sausage, sherry, and orange juice. Heat through and taste for salt and pepper. Serve garnished with egg and lemon and orange slices.

Serves 10 to 12

AFRICAN PEANUT SOUP

In West Africa, peanut soup is a staple which often includes shrimp or chicken and many different vegetables and wild herbs. In Nigeria, Ghana, Sierra Leone, and the Cameroons, the soup is often the center of the meal and is served with bowls of garnishes like cassava relish, papaya, pineapple, fried plantains, and grated coconut. Guests are always surprised and delighted with this somewhat unusual dish; the contrast of dry-roasted peanuts and fresh cilantro gives our rendition a particular sparkle.

---

1 large onion, chopped
1 red bell pepper, seeded and chopped
2 carrots, chopped
1 dried chili pepper, broken up
1 small potato, peeled and diced
4 cups Chicken Stock (page 20)
1 cup dry-roasted peanuts
Salt and pepper
¼ cup chopped dry-roasted peanuts
¼ cup coarsely chopped fresh cilantro leaves

In a large pot, combine onion, pepper, carrots, chili pepper, potato, and stock and bring to a boil. Reduce heat and simmer, uncovered, 30 minutes. Purée with whole peanuts in a blender or food processor. Taste for salt and pepper. Serve sprinkled with chopped peanuts and cilantro.

Serves 4 to 6

NOTES

NOTES

According to the dictionary, a soupçon is a small quantity or trace. In that spirit, we offer this array of little extras. They are meant to be dunked, sprinkled, drizzled, or floated and they always bring a touch of panache to a soup-centered meal.

⅔ cup all-purpose flour
⅔ cup yellow cornmeal
½ teaspoon salt
½ teaspoon ground cumin
2 teaspoons baking powder
2 tablespoons sugar
⅓ cup corn oil
2 large eggs, beaten
½ cup milk
1 cup corn kernels, fresh or frozen
* and thawed*
2 scallions, chopped
4 ounces grated cheddar cheese (optional)

Preheat the oven to 425 degrees F. Grease an 11-inch pie plate or baking dish. In a large bowl, combine dry ingredients. In a small bowl, beat oil, eggs, and milk. Stir into dry ingredients until well blended. Stir in corn and scallions just until evenly distributed. Pour mixture into pie plate and bake until golden brown, about 18 minutes. If using cheese, remove bread from oven and sprinkle cheese on top. Return to oven until cheese is melted or another 5 minutes. If cheese is not used, bake for a total time of 23 minutes or until golden brown. Let cool about 10 minutes and cut into wedges.

Serves 8

BREADSTICKS

1 package active dry yeast
1 tablespoon sugar or honey
½ cup warm water (about 110 degrees F)
2 cups bread flour
¾ cup whole wheat flour
1½ teaspoons salt
¼ cup milk, at room temperature
1 egg
Kosher salt, poppy seeds, and sesame seeds

Combine yeast with sugar and water. Let stand about 10 minutes or until foamy. In a large bowl, combine flours and 1 teaspoon of the salt. Stir in yeast mixture and then stir in milk. Work until a smooth and elastic dough is formed. Knead on a floured surface about 3 minutes. Put dough in oiled bowl, cover with plastic wrap, and let rise in a warm place until doubled in bulk, about 1 hour.

Preheat the oven to 400 degrees F and grease 2 baking sheets. Make the glaze by lightly beating egg with the remaining ½ teaspoon salt. Punch dough down and divide into 24 equal pieces. Roll each piece into an 8-inch rope. Place on baking sheets. Cover with plastic wrap and let rise in a warm spot, about 15 minutes. Mix together kosher salt, poppy seeds, and sesame seeds.

Brush bread sticks with egg glaze and sprinkle with seeds. Bake until golden brown, about 18 minutes. Remove from pan immediately and cool on racks.

Makes 24

DRY JACK CHEESE STRAWS

2 cups all-purpose flour
½ teaspoon salt
4 ounces (1 stick) cold butter, cut into small pieces
6 tablespoons sour cream
1 egg yolk, beaten
1 cup grated dry jack cheese
2 tablespoons paprika

In a food processor or with a pastry blender, combine flour, salt, and butter until crumbly. Add sour cream and mix until a rough dough forms. Form into a disk, wrap with plastic wrap, and refrigerate about 2 hours.

Preheat the oven to 400 degrees F. Butter 2 baking sheets. Roll dough out to a rectangle about ¼ inch thick. Brush with egg yolk and sprinkle with cheese and paprika. Cut dough into strips, about 6 x ¼ inch. Place on baking sheets and bake until straws are golden, about 12 minutes.

Makes about 50

SAVORY SCONES

2 cups all-purpose flour
1 tablespoon baking powder
½ teaspoon salt
½ cup grated Parmesan cheese
½ teaspoon dried oregano
½ cup chopped sundried tomatoes,
* oil-packed or dry*
1¼ cups heavy cream

Preheat the oven to 425 degrees F. In a large bowl, combine all the ingredients except cream. Stir in cream and mix until dough holds together. Turn out on floured surface and knead until dough becomes smoother, about 10 times. Pat into a 10-inch circle. Cut into 12 wedges and place on ungreased cookie sheet. Bake until golden brown, about 15 minutes.

Makes 12

PEPPERED POPOVERS

---

2 eggs
1 cup milk
1 tablespoon melted butter
¾ cup all-purpose flour
½ teaspoon salt
2 teaspoons freshly ground pepper
¼ teaspoon crushed red pepper flakes

Grease 8 muffin or popover molds. Mix eggs, milk, butter, flour, salt, black and red pepper until smooth. Half fill each cup with batter. Place in cold oven and turn heat to 450 degrees F. Bake for 15 minutes, turn heat down to 350 degrees F and bake another 12 minutes or until golden brown and puffed. Remove from pan and serve hot or warm.

Makes 8

HERBED FOCACCIA

1 package active dry yeast
1 teaspoon sugar or honey
½ cup warm water (about 110 degrees F)
1¼ cups bread flour
½ teaspoon dried oregano
½ teaspoon dried thyme
½ teaspoon dried rosemary
½ teaspoon salt
5 tablespoons olive oil
1 clove garlic, crushed

In a small bowl, combine yeast, sugar, and water. Let stand, about 10 minutes until foamy. In a large bowl, combine flour, half the oregano, thyme, rosemary, and salt. Add 1 tablespoon olive oil and yeast mixture and mix until dough forms. Turn out on a lightly floured surface and knead until smooth and elastic. Place in oiled bowl, cover with oiled plastic wrap, and let rise in a warm place until doubled in bulk, about 1 hour. Combine remaining oil with remaining herbs.

Preheat the oven to 425 degrees F and grease a 9 x 13-inch baking sheet. Punch dough down and turn out to lightly floured surface. Roll out to a 9 x 13-inch rectangle and place in prepared pan. Brush top with oil-herb mixture and sprinkle with crushed garlic. Dimple top with fingers. Bake until golden brown, about 8 minutes. Remove from pan and cut into 3-inch squares. Serve warm.

Makes 12

POLENTA-CHEESE CROUTONS

1 cup water
1 cup Chicken Stock (page 20)
¼ teaspoon salt
8 ounces polenta
2 tablespoons butter
1 cup (about 3 ounces) shredded cheese
   such as Parmesan, jack, asiago,
   or a mixture

Oil an 8 x 5-inch loaf pan. In a medium saucepan, bring water and stock to a boil. Add salt and slowly stir in polenta. Cook over low heat, stirring constantly until thick. This should take 10 to 15 minutes. Stir in butter and cheese. Pour into loaf pan and let harden at room temperature, about 45 minutes. Preheat the oven to 400 degrees F. Remove polenta from pan and slice about ½ inch thick. Cut slices into ½-inch cubes. Place on a cookie sheet, brush with oil, and bake, turning, until golden, about 12 minutes.

Makes about 3 cups

PEPPERY CHEESE CRISPS

½ pound longhorn or cheddar cheese, grated
4 ounces (1 stick) cold butter, cut into small pieces
½ cup all-purpose flour
¼ cup yellow cornmeal
1 to 2 jalapeño peppers, seeded and chopped
½ teaspoon salt
¼ teaspoon pepper

In a food processor or mixer, combine all the ingredients and mix until a ball of dough forms. Divide in half and place each half on a sheet of plastic wrap. Form each half into a log about 6 inches long and 1½ inches in diameter. Wrap in plastic wrap until firm enough to slice, about 2 hours. (Wrapped logs may be frozen up to 2 months.)

Preheat the oven to 400 degrees F. Slice logs ¼ inch thick and place about 2 inches apart on ungreased cookie sheet. Bake until edges are a golden brown, about 7 minutes. Remove to cooling rack to crisp and cool.

Makes about 50

SPICY BISCUIT THINS

2 tablespoons vegetable oil
2 shallots, chopped
2 cloves garlic, minced
¼ cup prepared mustard
½ cup water
1½ cups all-purpose flour
½ cup whole wheat flour
⅛ teaspoon cayenne
1 tablespoon baking powder
½ teaspoon salt
6 tablespoons cold butter, cut into small pieces

Preheat the oven to 450 degrees F. Heat oil in a small skillet and cook shallots and garlic until golden brown, about 6 minutes. Let cool slightly. In a small bowl, combine shallot mixture with mustard and water.

In a medium bowl, combine flours, cayenne, baking powder, and salt. Cut in butter until mixture resembles cornmeal. Stir in the mustard mixture until it forms a soft dough. Gather into a ball and knead gently on floured surface. Roll out to about ⅛ inch thick. Cut out rounds with 2-inch cutter and place on an ungreased baking sheet. Gather scraps and reroll. Cut rounds again. Bake about 10 minutes or until golden brown. Remove to cooling racks to crisp and cool.

Makes about 70

CROUTONS

2 cups ¼-inch crustless bread cubes from
  close-grained bread
4 tablespoons vegetable oil, butter, or
  a combination
Herbs and spices such as garlic, oregano,
  thyme, sage, curry, or a mixture (optional)

Let bread cubes dry out by spreading on a cookie sheet in a single layer for 1 to 2 hours. Heat oil in a large skillet over medium-high heat. Add herbs or spices, if using, to oil while heating. Sauté the bread, tossing and stirring, until golden brown on all sides. Drain on paper towels.

Makes 2 cups

CROSTINI

12 thick slices day-old country-style bread
Olive oil
1 clove garlic, cut in half

Preheat the oven to 375 degrees F. Lightly brush both sides of bread with oil. Place on a cookie sheet and toast until golden brown, about 8 minutes per side. While still warm, rub each side of crostini with cut clove of garlic.

Makes 12

TOPPINGS FOR CROSTINI

The following toppings will add an interesting flavorful dimension to the crostini that accompanies your soup. While most of the toppings may be made in advance, they should be spread on crostini just before serving.

OLIVADA

In a food processor or blender, combine 1 cup pitted, imported black or green olives, 2 cloves garlic, ¼ teaspoon thyme, 1 tablespoon lemon juice, and 4 tablespoons olive oil; process until a rough paste forms. Taste for salt and pepper. *Makes 1 cup*

ROUILLE

In a food processor or blender, combine 1 egg yolk, 1 teaspoon lemon juice, 2 cloves garlic, 2 roasted and peeled red bell peppers, 1 slice crustless white bread, and ¼ teaspoon crushed red pepper flakes until fairly smooth. While machine is running, slowly add ½ cup olive oil and process until thick. Taste for salt and pepper. *Makes about 1 cup*

Caution: Raw egg yolks may contain salmonella bacteria, which can cause food poisoning.

AÏOLI

In a food processor or blender, combine 1 egg yolk, 1 teaspoon mustard, 1 teaspoon fresh lemon juice, and 4 cloves garlic; process until smooth. Slowly add 1 cup olive oil until mixture becomes thick. Taste for salt and pepper. *Makes 1 cup*

Caution: Raw egg yolks may contain salmonella bacteria, which can cause food poisoning.

PESTO

In a food processor or blender, combine 2 cups basil leaves, 3 cloves garlic, ½ teaspoon dried oregano, ⅓ cup toasted pine nuts (page 31), ⅓ cup grated Parmesan cheese, and ½ cup olive oil; process until a rough paste is formed. Taste for salt and pepper. *Makes 1 cup*

SUNDRIED TOMATO PESTO

In a food processor or blender, combine ½ cup soaked or oil-packed sundried tomatoes, 2 cloves garlic, ½ teaspoon dried oregano, ½ teaspoon dried thyme, ¼ cup basil leaves, ¼ cup grated Parmesan cheese, and ⅓ cup olive oil; process until a rough paste is formed. Taste for salt and pepper. *Makes about ¼ cup*

4 small (6-inch) pita breads
2 tablespoons olive oil or melted butter
¼ teaspoon salt

Preheat the oven to 350 degrees F. With small sharp scissors, cut pita breads in half making two 6-inch discs. Brush unbaked surface of each half with oil and sprinkle with salt. Cut each half into 6 wedges. Place on cookie sheet and bake until golden and crisp, about 10 minutes.

Makes 48

OMELETTE THREADS

2 eggs
1 tablespoon all-purpose flour
1 tablespoon potato starch
2 tablespoons milk
½ teaspoon salt
¼ teaspoon freshly ground pepper
Oil

In a small bowl, combine eggs, flour, potato starch, milk, salt, and pepper and stir until smooth. Let batter rest about 30 minutes. Lightly oil an 8-inch nonstick skillet. Pour in enough batter just to cover bottom of pan, about ¼ cup. Cook until pale and slightly bubbly. Flip to other side and cook another 30 seconds. Remove from pan. Continue with remaining batter and stack omelets. Cut into very thin strips. Float or stir into soup.

Serves 6 to 8

SOUPSWIRLS

Everyone loves toppings—sundaes with a cherry on top, pie with a dollop of whipped cream, curry with chutney. Like toppings, these soupswirls are the final touch that finishes things off, providing a little extra zing at the end. Here are some of our favorites.

SAFFRON SWIRL

In a medium bowl, combine ½ teaspoon saffron, soaked in 1 tablespoon hot water, and ½ cup heavy cream. Let stand 10 minutes. Whip just until lightly thickened. Swirl in fish or potato soups. *Makes ½ cup*

RED PEPPER SWIRL

In a food processor or blender, combine peeled and seeded roasted red pepper (page 31), ⅛ teaspoon cayenne, ½ teaspoon sugar, ½ teaspoon salt, and ¼ cup yogurt. Purée until smooth. Swirl into bean or fish soups. *Makes about ¼ cup*

CILANTRO-MINT SWIRL

In a food processor or blender, combine ½ cup fresh cilantro, ½ jalapeño pepper, seeded, 8 mint leaves, 1 tablespoon brown sugar, and ½ teaspoon salt. Process to make a rough paste and stir into yogurt. Swirl into any mild-flavored cream soup. *Makes about 1 cup*

PARSLEY-ANCHOVY SWIRL

In a food processor or blender, combine ½ cup parsley leaves, 4 rinsed anchovy fillets, 1 teaspoon fresh lemon juice, and 8 tablespoons room-temperature butter. Process until smooth. Refrigerate, well wrapped, until ready to use. Swirl 1 or 2 teaspoons into hot vegetable soup. *Makes about ½ cup*

TARRAGON-CHIVE SWIRL

In a food processor or blender, combine 3 tablespoons fresh tarragon leaves or 1 teaspoon dried tarragon, ¼ cup chopped chives, 1 teaspoon Dijon mustard, ¼ teaspoon salt, ¼ teaspoon freshly ground pepper, and ½ cup sour cream. Process until well blended. Swirl into meat and vegetable soups. *Makes ½ cup*

HORSERADISH-DILL SWIRL

In a food processor or blender, combine 3 tablespoons freshly grated or commercially prepared horseradish, 2 tablespoons fresh dill, ¼ teaspoon salt, and 6 ounces cream cheese. Process until well blended. Swirl into fish soups. *Makes about ½ cup*

SUNDRIED TOMATO SWIRL

In a food processor or blender, combine ¼ cup drained oil-packed sundried tomatoes, 1 teaspoon fresh thyme or ½ teaspoon dried thyme, 10 fresh basil leaves, 1 clove garlic, 3 tablespoons Parmesan cheese, ⅛ teaspoon salt, ⅛ teaspoon freshly ground pepper, and ½ cup heavy cream. Process until smooth. Swirl into vegetable soups. *Makes about ¾ cup*

INFUSED OILS

Intensely flavored infused oils, when drizzled over a bowl of soup, explode with the flavors and aromas of fruits, vegetables, herbs, and spices. You can make infused oil from any food that has been dried and ground to a powder such as herbs, spices, mushrooms, onions, and tomatoes, or with citrus zest.

ROSEMARY OIL

Mix ¼ cup dried rosemary with ¼ cup water. Pour into a wide-mouthed jar, add ½ cup olive oil, close jar, and shake to distribute the ingredients. Let stand at room temperature, preferably in a cool dark place, for 3 days. After 1 day the rosemary will have settled to the bottom. After 3 days ladle out the oil to a clean jar and discard the rosemary mixture at bottom. Store as you would olive oil. Sprinkle on fish or lamb soups. *Makes ½ cup*

PROVENÇAL OIL

Combine 1 tablespoon *each* dried rosemary, dried basil, dried thyme, and dried tarragon with ¼ cup water. Pour into a wide-mouthed jar, add ½ cup olive oil, close jar, and shake. Continue as for Rosemary Oil. Sprinkle on vegetable or tomato soups. *Makes ½ cup*

MUSHROOM OIL

Pulverize ¼ cup dried mushrooms in a blender or spice grinder and combine with ¼ cup water in a wide-mouthed jar. Add ½ cup canola oil, close jar, and shake. Continue as for Rosemary Oil. Sprinkle on vegetable soups. *Makes ½ cup*

SANTA FE OIL

Combine 2 teaspoons crushed red pepper, ¼ cup dried cilantro or parsley, 1 tablespoon lime zest with ¼ cup water in a wide-mouthed jar. Add ½ cup canola, safflower, or vegtable oil, close jar, and shake. Continue as for Rosemary Oil. Sprinkle on bean soups. *Makes about ½ cup*

TOMATO-SAFFRON OIL

In a food processor or blender, pulverize ¼ cup sundried tomatoes (not oil-packed). Combine with 1 tablespoon saffron powder and ¼ cup water in a wide-mouthed jar. Add ½ cup canola oil, close jar, and shake. Proceed as with Rosemary Oil. Sprinkle on fish soups. *Makes about ½ cup*

CURRY OIL

Combine ¼ cup curry powder, 2 tablespoons ground coriander, and ¼ cup water in a wide-mouthed jar. Add ½ cup canola, safflower, or vegetable oil and shake. Proceed as with Rosemary Oil. Sprinkle on vegetable or lamb soups. *Makes about ½ cup*

CITRUS OIL

Combine 2 tablespoons orange, lemon, or lime zest, or a combination and ½ cup canola, safflower, or vegetable oil in a jar with lid. Let stand 3 days in a cool dark place. Strain oil, discarding zest. Sprinkle on fruit or shellfish soups. *Makes ½ cup*

NOTES

NOTES

TABLE OF EQUIVALENTS

The exact equivalents in the following tables have been rounded for convenience.

US/UK

oz	ounce
lb	pound
in	inch
ft	foot
tbl	tablespoon
fl oz	fluid ounce
qt	quart

METRIC

g	gram
kg	kilogram
mm	millimeter
cm	centimeter
ml	milliliter
l	liter

WEIGHTS

US/UK	METRIC
1 oz	30 g
2 oz	60 g
3 oz	90 g
4 oz (¼ lb)	125 g
5 oz (⅓ lb)	155 g
6 oz	185 g
7 oz	220 g
8 oz (½ lb)	250 g
10 oz	315 g
12 oz (¾ lb)	375 g
14 oz	440 g
16 oz (1 lb)	500 g
1½ lb	750 g
2 lb	1 kg
3 lb	1.5 kg

LIQUIDS

US	METRIC	UK
2 tbl	30 ml	1 fl oz
¼ cup	60 ml	2 fl oz
⅓ cup	80 ml	3 fl oz
½ cup	125 ml	4 fl oz
⅔ cup	160 ml	5 fl oz
¾ cup	180 ml	6 fl oz
1 cup	250 ml	8 fl oz
1½ cups	375 ml	12 fl oz
2 cups	1 l	32 fl oz

OVEN TEMPERATURES

FAHRENHEIT	CELSIUS	GAS
250	120	½
275	140	1
300	150	2
325	160	3
350	180	4
375	190	5
400	200	6
425	220	7
450	230	8
475	240	9
500	260	10

LENGTH MEASURES

⅛ in	3 mm
¼ in	6 mm
½ in	12 mm
1 in	2.5 cm
2 in	5 cm
3 in	7.5 cm
4 in	10 cm
5 in	13 cm
6 in	15 cm
7 in	18 cm
8 in	20 cm
9 in	23 cm
10 in	25 cm
11 in	28 cm
12 in/1 ft	30 cm

EQUIVALENTS FOR COMMONLY USED INGREDIENTS

WHOLE-WHEAT (WHOLE MEAL) FLOUR

3 tbl	1 oz	30 g
½ cup	2 oz	60 g
⅔ cup	3 oz	90 g
1 cup	4 oz	125 g
1¼ cups	5 oz	155 g
1⅔ cups	7 oz	210 g
1¾ cups	8 oz	250 g

RAISINS/CURRANTS/SEMOLINA

¼ cup	1 oz	30 g
⅓ cup	2 oz	60 g
½ cup	3 oz	90 g
¾ cup	4 oz	125 g
1 cup	5 oz	155 g

DRIED BEANS

¼ cup	1 ½ oz	45 g
⅓ cup	2 oz	60 g
½ cup	3 oz	90 g
¾ cup	5 oz	155 g
1 cup	6 oz	185 g
1¼ cups	8 oz	250 g
1½ cups	12 oz	375 g

JAM/HONEY

2 tbl	2 oz	60 g
¼ cup	3 oz	90 g
½ cup	5 oz	155 g
¾ cup	8 oz	250 g
1 cup	11 oz	345 g

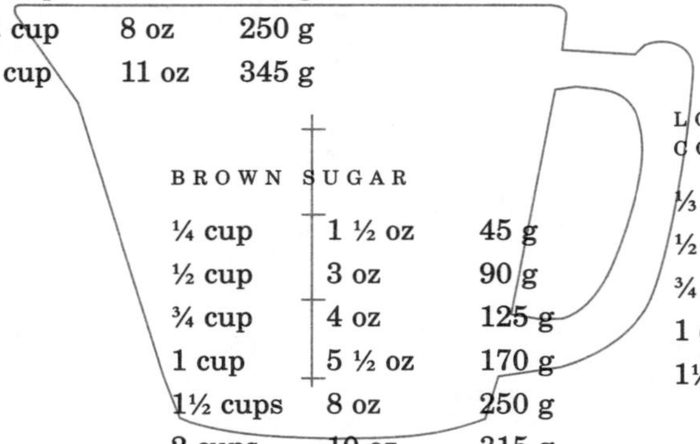

WHITE SUGAR

¼ cup	2 oz	60 g
⅓ cup	3 oz	90 g
½ cup	4 oz	125 g
¾ cup	6 oz	185 g
1 cup	8 oz	250 g
1½ cups	12 oz	375 g
2 cups	1 lb	500 g

BROWN SUGAR

¼ cup	1 ½ oz	45 g
½ cup	3 oz	90 g
¾ cup	4 oz	125 g
1 cup	5 ½ oz	170 g
1½ cups	8 oz	250 g
2 cups	10 oz	315 g

LONG-GRAIN RICE/CORNMEAL

⅓ cup	2 oz	60 g
½ cup	2 ½ oz	75 g
¾ cup	4 oz	125 g
1 cup	5 oz	155 g
1½ cups	8 oz	250 g

GRATED PARMESAN/ROMANO CHEESE

¼ cup	1 oz	30 g
½ cup	2 oz	60 g
¾ cup	3 oz	90 g
1 cup	4 oz	125 g
1⅓ cups	5 oz	155 g
2 cups	7 oz	220 g

ALL-PURPOSE (PLAIN) FLOUR/DRIED BREAD CRUMBS/CHOPPED NUTS

¼ cup	1 oz	30 g
⅓ cup	1 ½ oz	45 g
½ cup	2 oz	60 g
¾ cup	3 oz	90 g
1 cup	4 oz	125 g
1½ cups	6 oz	185 g
2 cups	8 oz	250 g

ROLLED OATS

⅓ cup	1 oz	30 g
⅔ cup	2 oz	60 g
1 cup	3 oz	90 g
1½ cups	4 oz	125 g
2 cups	5 oz	155 g